Robin + Larry
Smith
(612)-419-6507

Pickleball

The Ultimate Beginner's Guide to Fun, Friends, and Strategies

Dan Janal

Forewords by Hall of Famers
Steve Paranto and Steve Dawson

With New Yorker Cartoonist
Lisa Rothstein

© Daniel S. Janal, 2024. All Rights Reserved.

Cartoons © by Lisa Rothstein, 2024. All Rights Reserved.

Images cannot be reproduced under any circumstances.

Cover photo courtesy of Ann Laurent.

Pictured on the cover:
Anna Peterson (front left) and Tim Laurent (front right)
David Dutrieuille (back left) and Katie Easter (back right)

Editorial content can be reproduced only with written permission by Daniel S. Janal.

All rights reserved. No portion of these materials may be reproduced or transmitted in any form or by any means, electronic or mechanical, including photocopying, recording, or any information storage and retrieval system without prior written consent from the publisher.

While all attempts have been made to verify the information provided in this publication, neither the Author nor the Publisher assumes any responsibility for errors, omissions, or contradictory interpretations of the subject matter herein.

The reader assumes all responsibility for his/her own actions in regard to any items discussed in this book. Adherence to all applicable laws and regulations, federal, state, and local, governing the use of any product or service described in this manual in the US or any other jurisdiction is the sole responsibility of the reader. The publisher and author assume no responsibility or liability whatsoever on behalf of the reader of these materials. Any perceived slights of specific people or organizations are unintentional.

The author is a compensated affiliate for some products mentioned in this book. He recommends only those products he'd buy and use so you are assured the recommendations are honest.

Dedicated to my wonderful wife, Susan Tracy.

10 9 8 7 6 5 4 3 2 1

Published by Janal Communications

Printed in the United States of America

Special discounts for bulk sales
are available. Please contact
publisher@PickleballPublishingCompany.com

Table of Contents

Foreword by Steve Dawson 1
Foreword by Steve Paranto 3
Meet Your Coaches 7
Letter from the Author 13
Welcome to Pickleball, an International Sensation 15
A Brief History 29
PART 1 - Get into the Game 31
Chapter 1 - Pickleball—The Basics 33
Chapter 2 - The Lay of the Land 37
Chapter 3 - Two Rules You Absolutely Need to Know 39
Chapter 4 - Terms You Need to Know 43
Chapter 5 - How to Keep Score 47
Chapter 6 - Where Do I Stand? 51
Chapter 7 - The Five Stages of a Rally 53
Chapter 8 - After-Game Etiquette 69
PART 2 - How to Not Look Like a Newbie 71
Chapter 9 - Getting to Know You: How to Meet 73
Other Newbies

Chapter 10 - I Want to Play with YOU! Be a Good 81
Pickleball Partner

Chapter 11 - Dress for Success: What Equipment 91
Do I Need?

Chapter 12 - Where Can I Play, and What Should 99
I Pay?

Chapter 13 - How to Get into a Game: Open Play 107
for Everyone!

Chapter 14 - Playing at Your Level 113

Chapter 15 - The Pickleball Code: Unwritten Rules 121
for Success

Chapter 16 - Mind Games: Keep a Positive Attitude 129

Chapter 17 - The Body Game: Don't Get Hurt! 137

Chapter 18 - Ready Position/ Athletic Stance 149

Chapter 19 - Footwork 153

Chapter 20 - Fully Armed 155

Chapter 21 - The Eyes Have It 157

Chapter 22 - Shake Hands with Your New Best 159
Friend: Your Paddle

PART 3 - Get Strategic 161

Chapter 23 - The 75% Paradox: Pickleball's Dirty 167
Little Secret

Chapter 24 - The Kitchen Is Cooking! 171

Chapter 25 - Beat the Bangers! 173

Chapter 26 - Pickleball, Anyone? Tips for Tennis 175
Players

PART 4 - Get Better 177

Chapter 27 - What Level Are You? 179

Chapter 28 - Diary of a Successful Pickleball Player 181

Chapter 29 - What to Expect When You Attend 187
a Lesson or a Clinic

Chapter 30 - Going from Good to Great on the................ 189
Pickleball Court: Get a Coach

Chapter 31 - Perfect Practice Makes Perfect: Get 195
a Drill Partner

Chapter 32 - Lights! Camera! Action: How to Get........... 203
the Most from a Video

Chapter 33 - Easy Solutions to Common Problems......... 205

Chapter 34 - Pay It Forward... 213

Pickleball Gift Store.. *219*

Pickleball Products *221*

"Pickleball Saved My Life!" *223*

Share Pickleball: The Ultimate Beginner's Guide to Fun, ... *225*
Friends, and Strategies With Your Members!

Acknowledgements *229*

About the Author Dan Janal *231*

About the Cartoonist Lisa Rothstein.. *233*

Foreword
by Steve Dawson

Pickleball builds community.

A lot of people come by themselves for open play. Our rules are inclusive. So, someone who shows up here for pickleball gets invited into a game, introduced to a new person, and makes friends on the pickleball court. And then it's just a matter of time until that person's entire social calendar is filled up with pickleball people and pickleball friends he or she has met here at the club. That's how it works.

The nature of the sport is friendly. But as a private club owner, I always have to be out there encouraging players so that we don't get too many overly win-friendly people that have to win at all costs. We want more of an inclusive and inviting environment. That's what we work at.

One of my open play rules is, "BE KIND. It Matters!"

That's the most important rule.

Everyone should realize pickleball is a game. Realize it's for everyone's enjoyment. Realize that no one really cares who won or lost. The real "win" is how many nice people you've met and how gracious your attitude was. When I'm done playing, I don't care who I beat or who I lost to. It's who was nice and who was unfriendly. That's really what matters.

Steve Dawson
Encinitas, California
Owner, Bobby Riggs Racquet and Paddle
(Winner of Top Pickleball Club of 2020)

- One of the Top Pickleball Players in the world
- A highly celebrated and sought-after pickleball coach
- Multiple U.S. Open and U.S. National Pickleball Champion
- 2-Time Canadian National Champion and Huntsman World Pickleball Champion
- Co-founder of ProKennex Pickleball, Picklepalooza, and Boost Pickleball Camps

Foreword
by Steve Paranto

Why is pickleball the fastest-growing sport in America?

It's the people.

The people and the social aspect are just as important as the game.

We're close together when we play. We play the play with partners. We switch partners all the time. Almost every game. So, we meet new people. We become friends with new people.

Compare pickleball to a day on the golf course. You're with three other people all day. But in pickleball, you might be with sixteen people in a two-hour or three-hour session. You get a chance to mix with so many different people.

We have common goals. All the players are working hard on their game. Usually, you'll wind up being friends with the people you've just met. So, it's great to work on those common goals together.

In the classes I teach, people will leave the class getting phone numbers from others so they can meet and play with them.

Playing pickleball is fun.

You know, it's just fun.

The rallies are fun. More so than other racket sports. The rallies last a lot longer than any other racket sports.

That's why you hear people laughing at the pickleball courts. You don't hear people laughing on the tennis courts very often, do you?

In pickleball, it seems like everyone's just having fun. I went to nationals and heard Dave Weinbach making jokes on the court. You can tell he's having fun with the other people on the court. It's not just because he's beating them but because of the social aspect.

I don't think you see that much fun among players in other pro sports.

And, of course, you can enjoy pickleball the first day you play.

I've met the nicest people in the world. Every so often, I have to pinch myself with the astonishing popularity of this sport.

Pickleball has so many things going for it.

Isn't it time you got into the game?

Steve Paranto
Portland, Oregon

Accomplishments

- Currently teaching at RECS Pickleball Cub in Clackamas, Oregon
- Longest run as a tournament player from 1974 until the present
- Multinational champion at 5.0 level
- Won at the 5.0 level in six different decades
- Coached many national champions
- Helped my father create the first composite pickleball paddle and designed the first oversized paddle
- Teaching pickleball since 1979
- Inducted into the Pickleball Hall of Fame in 2019

Meet Your Coaches

In this book, you will meet more than a dozen coaches from all over the U.S. I could not have written this book without their help, guidance, support, and camaraderie! I'd like to introduce them to you here, so we don't have to slow down the book by reintroducing them each time you see their names.

In some cases, interviews were shortened for conciseness and clarity. Any resulting unintended errors are the author's.

They are:

Steve Paranto is a Hall of Fame member for his contributions to the sport. Inventor of the drop serve. Co-inventor of the honeycomb paddle with his father. Physical Education teacher for more than 30 years. The only person to win championships in each of six decades, starting in the 1970s. He lives in a house with two indoor pickleball courts in Beaver Creek, Oregon. sparanto@comcast.net

Steve Dawson is the owner of Bobby Riggs Paddle and Racket Club in Encinitas, California (Winner of Top Pickleball

Club of 2020). He is one of the top pickleball players in the world and a highly celebrated and sought-after pickleball coach. He's a multiple U.S. Open and U.S. National Pickleball Champion, a Two-Time Canadian National Champion and Huntsman World Pickleball Champion, and co-founder of ProKennex Pickleball, Picklepalooza, and Boost Pickleball Camps. www.bobbyriggs.net/ steve@bobbyriggs.net

Tim Laurent got involved in Pickleball to lose a little weight. "I had no idea what an awesome sport I stumbled across. Coaching allows me to exercise my passion for teaching!" He's a certified instructor of Pickleball Coaching International (PCI) and has more than four years of experience coaching pickleball. He was co-head coach of the AAU Pickleball Junior Olympic Games. He teaches the 5 Ps of Pickleball: "Patience, Positioning, Placement, Power, PRACTICE." He lives in the western suburbs of Minneapolis.

Coach Tim Laurent spreads the joy
of pickleball everywhere he drives.

Spencer Laurent is the founder and CEO of Pickleball TV, based in Encinitas, California. He is a TV commentator on pickleball tournaments and a 5.0 player. He has been doing live pickleball productions for Professional Pickleball Association (PPA), Major League Pickleball (MLP), and Association of Pickleball Professionals (APP). He is currently a producer for PPA, working at the Tennis Channel. He is Coach Tim's son. thepickleballtv@gmail.com

Clinton Young is a Professional Pickleball Registry (PPR) certified Pickleball Coach based in Austin, Texas and San Diego, California. He's a Pro Pickleball Commentator and Founder of Pickleball4Life.com. He is a Global Courage Speaker and full-time RVer, traveling the U.S. with his wife, speaking, and leading Pickleball-inspired events for corporations, schools, and charities to inspire mental, emotional, physical, and spiritual well-being in the community. See Clinton speak and follow him on Instagram and Facebook @ClintonSpeaks and online at ClintonYoung.com and www.Pickleball4Life.org.

Barrett Kincheloe is a PPR and International Pickleball Teaching Professional Association (IPTPA) certified instructor, writer, podcaster, and YouTuber. He is the owner of Pickleball Kitchen, whose goal is to help as many people as possible with pickleball. He lives in McKinney, Texas, just outside of Dallas. www.PickleballKitchen.com

M.J. Miniati is the founder and "Director of Fitness and Fun" of More Joy Pickleball based in Narragansett, Rhode Island. MJ is a Professional Pickleball Registry (PPR) certified Coach with a Master's Degree in Sports Management from the University of Massachusetts. As a D1AA scholarship swimmer at the University of Rhode Island, she has coached numerous sports throughout her athletic career prior to discovering the social and physical benefits of Pickleball while vacationing in Naples, Florida. She has been sharing the joys and benefits of Pickleball since 2015 throughout Rhode Island and neighboring states. More Joy Pickleball runs leagues, clinics, lessons, tournaments, and excursions. Proceeds from the Alex's Smile tournaments benefit MeetingStreet – an organization for children with special needs. She can be reached at 401-954-4038, MJ@MoreJoyPickleball.com, or MoreJoyFit.com. You can also follow More Joy Pickleball on Facebook and Instagram.

Jim "Jimbo" Cohen is a 4.0+ U.S.A. Pickleball Association (USAPA) ranked player and frequent tournament medalist in both doubles and singles. He is an IPTPA-certified national coach, rating specialist, and referee. He is Co-Founder/Honorary Chair of Mexico Pickleball and Founding Member, Board of Directors of the World Pickleball Federation/Association, National Pickleball (NP). He offers coaching and clinics in Mexico, Florida, Utah, and Minnesota. spiritofthehummingbird.com

Stacie Townsend, founder of ThePickler.com, a pickleball content and pickleball resource that tries to promote and grow the sport. www.ThePickler.com

Pam Rauber is a pickleball teacher in North Georgia.

Daniel McConnell, a pickleball coach in Eden Prairie, Minnesota. mcdunthat@yahoo.com

Charlie Ball has been a member of the United States Professional Tennis Association (USPTA) for over eight years. He taught tennis for years but has fallen in love with pickleball. After graduating with a degree in physical education from Purdue University, Charlie is now fully engrossed in Pickleball and coaches both sports professionally. He's a pickleball coach at Bobby Riggs Racket and Paddle Club in Encinitas, California. 3.0topro@gmail.com.

Katie Easter is Minnesota Lifetime Pickleball Lead. keaster952@gmail.com

CJ Johnson, co-founder of We Are Pickleball, is a professional three-sport athlete and coach who has spent her entire adult life earning a living from playing and coaching sports. She believes, "Good pickleball is not just technique, it's the mind and body working holistically."
http://www.wearepickleball.com.

"Mike's been obsessed since he discovered pickleball."

Letter from the Author

Pickleball Paradise

I'll never forget the first time I played pickleball.

It was easy and fun!

For the first time in my life, I felt like I could play a sport and be good at it! Those are proud words from someone who was usually among the last to be picked for any game from elementary school through college!

I met people who didn't care if they won or lost.

Having fun was the goal. Who cared what the score was?

If I get better at a skill or meet a new friend, I consider that a day well spent on the pickleball court.

Do you feel the same way?

That's part of the joy of pickleball.

Dan Janal

Welcome to Pickleball, an International Sensation

Pick up your paddle!

You are joining the fastest-growing sport in America!

Pickleball is a fun and easy-to-learn sport that combines elements of tennis, badminton, and ping pong. You can learn to play the sport in less than 30 minutes and have fun in the process. It doesn't matter if it rains or shines. You can play indoors or outdoors.

Pickleball is a great sport for all ages and skill levels. This sport is a great way to exercise and have fun with friends. If you're just starting out, taking a few lessons to get a feel for the game and learning the rules before jumping into a competitive match is a good idea.

Over the past few years, pickleball has evolved from a niche sport to an international sensation. More than 36.5 million people played pickleball from August 2021 to August 2022, according to a new report by the Association of Pickleball Professionals. That's up an amazing number of 5 million players in 2021. Insiders expect the sport to attract 40 million people by 2030. That number should easily be eclipsed by the time you read this book.

Insiders expect the sport to attract 40 million people by 2030. People in 58 countries play pickleball, according to the International Federation of Pickleball. Promoters are lobbying to have pickleball played in the Olympics and Paralympics. ESPN broadcasts pickleball tournaments, offering tens of thousands of dollars in prize money. Billionaires are forming leagues and buying teams. Articles in major media appear nearly every day with headlines like, "Can Pickleball Save America?"

Courts for recreational players are being built every day. Many tennis courts are being converted or re-striped for pickleball. Pickleball-only facilities measuring 30,000 square feet are being built with restaurants, bars, and viewing areas. They have names like "Chicken N Pickle," "Lucky Shots," "Mega Pickle & Pong," and "Smash Park." Life Time, one of the largest health clubs in the nation, plans to expand its 235 dedicated pickleball courts to more than 600 by the end of 2023.

Now is the right time for you to get in the game!

The Joy of Pickleball

To the people who play, pickleball is not just a game.

People who play pickleball describe it as an addiction or an obsession. The game is that much fun!

What makes it fun?

The fact you are meeting new people, forming a community, and getting exercise.

Pickleball Is Not Just for Old Folks Anymore

Let's dispel the myth that pickleball is "tennis for old people."

At any court, you will see people of all ages playing together. It's not unusual to see muscular teenagers lose to little old ladies who know a thing or two about strategy. The average age of a pickleball player is 38 years old, according to U.S.A. Pickleball, with each major age group fairly evenly represented. Celebrities like Kim Kardashian, Ellen DeGeneres, George Clooney, Larry David, and Matthew Perry play pickleball. So do athletes like Michael Phelps and Larry Fitzgerald. The list of newcomers reads like a Who's Who of Hall of Fame Athletes and A-List celebrities. Everyone is getting into the game!

And, of course, millions of regular people play pickleball.

"I'm loving pickleball! I've been playing since January. I became addicted quickly," said Ashley Lanahan, an acupuncturist in Leucadia, California. She played high school varsity tennis doubles.

"Addiction" is a word frequently used to describe people who play pickleball. Many people play more than four times a week!

Coach Tim commented, "I believe pickleball will be the biggest sport in the history of the world. And I believe that for a reason. There aren't any 80-year-old soccer players, or at least, not too many active ones. Whether you're eight or 80, it doesn't make a difference."

"Give Mark some space. He just got his butt kicked by a 78-year-old grandma."

People of all ages are picking up paddles and making pickleball the fastest-growing sport in America. It is easy to see why:

- You don't need to be the fastest like in the sport of running.

- You don't have to be tall, like in basketball.

- You don't have to run forever, like in soccer.

- You don't have to be built like a football player.

- Compared to tennis, you can be less of an athlete—less running, less power, less emphasis on serving, less backswing.

Pickleball is the great equalizer of a sport. The rules make competition fair.

- Pickleball is easy to play. You can learn to play a game in just a few minutes. Of course, pickleball will take longer to master—just like any activity.

- Pickleball is fun! Many people say they are addicted to pickleball and play it several times a week.

- Pickleball is social. People like to play pickleball to meet new people. Adults find it harder to make new friends, but pickleball makes meeting new people with similar interests very easy. Couples who met on pickleball courts have gotten married on pickleball courts.

- Pickleball is a great equalizer. You don't have to be strong, fast, or muscular to play well. Unlike tennis, power is not essential. It is one of the few sports—perhaps only sport—where women can play competitively with men and where older adults regularly trounce young people.

You need to be alert, patient, and strategic. All the while, you are getting exercise and making new friends.

That's why 80-year-old grandmothers can play—and beat—17-year-old kids.

That's why men and women can play together on an equal footing.

That's why parents and children can have fun together.

People with varying abilities can enjoy the sport. I've played with:

- A guy in an adapted sports wheelchair. He has a killer serve in which he pivoted his wheelchair 360 degrees to build a powerful momentum.
- A guy with Parkinson's. He didn't run well, but he had a terrific serve!
- A retired teacher in her 90s. She ran me ragged.
- A rhinestone-bedazzled beauty queen with a boombox and a chihuahua. She was a terrific partner and an all-around nice person.

Coach M.J. said, "Nerdy geeks should be playing. Almost anyone can play. It doesn't matter how well you play. It matters that you play. For the most part, pickleball is a welcoming sport."

You'll meet all kinds of people.

You'll get exercise.

For social players, it's all about having fun!

No wonder why pickleball is snowballing!

Pickleball Is a Family Activity

On any court, you are likely to see families playing together.

"Pickleball gives us an opportunity to get together. In fact, three of us have sons and sons-in-law that play together. There aren't many sports where we can play together and be competitive. He gets to more balls, but I know more strategy. That's fun. It doesn't matter if you are old or young, skinny or heavy. You can all play and play well," said Don Clements, a pickleball enthusiast and State Farm Insurance Agent in Lee's Summit, Missouri, a suburb of Kansas City.

Coach Paranto said, "I often play with fathers and sons and moms and daughters. You can't do that in soccer. You can't have a 60-year-old mom playing with a 30-year-old daughter and be competitive. I mean, you could play, but it wouldn't be pretty. Pickleball can be very competitive with those age groups."

How This Book Will Help You!

This book is for all the new players who want to make friends and have fun playing pickleball—but who might feel out of place, intimidated, and confused.

This book provides everything the beginning pickleball player needs to know to get started. This book doesn't cover every stroke, strategy, and situation in pickleball. However, by using the ideas in this book, you'll be amazed at how much fun you'll have, how many new friends you will meet, and how much better you will feel.

When I asked people in Facebook pickleball groups what they wished they knew when they were starting to play, they didn't say "the rules," "how to serve," or "strategy." They wanted to know how to find places to play, make friends, find community, and meet players at their skill level.

When you read this book, you'll be more confident when you go to a court because you'll know what to say and do. You'll be more self-assured because you'll know how to play the game and improve your skills.

You'll quickly find:

- Friends to play with, so you'll never feel out of place.
- How to play nicely with others, so you fit in with any group and the other players will want to play with you.
- How to fit in with the cool kids, jocks, and even the cliques—no matter their age.

- Fun drills, so you improve quickly.

- How to get the most out of lessons with coaches so your money will be well spent.

- Tools to mark your progress so you can see how far you've come!

Let's not forget the emotional benefits you'll gain by reading this book. You'll feel:

- More confident because you'll know how to act, what to say, and how to play the game.

- More empowered because you'll learn how to avoid mistakes.

- More relaxed and at ease because you'll know the official rules and the "unwritten rules."

Of course, you'll learn how to play the game on a basic level. You'll know:

- The most important rules you must understand, so you play the game correctly.

- Where to stand and what to do so you can hold your own on the court.

- How to keep score, which confuses many new players because of pickleball's unique rules.

- Critical strategies for new players so you play more skillfully.

You'll want to read this book if you are:

- Overwhelmed by online articles and videos.

- Confused by getting the wrong advice from well-meaning friends.

How You Can Get the Most from This Book

You will find this book fun to read because it is packed with illustrations, diagrams, pictures, cartoons, assessments, journals, and fill-in-the-blank fun sheets, with advice from America's top coaches and other new players like you. You'll also see links to videos so you can get a deeper explanation along with the visual elements when you see someone play. Words can do only so much.

This book has four sections. You can read the sections in any order.

1. **Get in the Game.** This is the section where you learn to play pickleball. You'll learn the essential rules and how to keep score, which frustrates many new players. You'll walk through all the stages of the rally, so you'll know where to stand and how to play the game properly. You'll see links to videos so you can see exactly what to do.

2. **How to Not Look Like Newbie.** You'll learn all about the basics of the social aspects of the game. You'll learn how to find people to play with and find places to play.

You'll learn the game's etiquette—and the unwritten rules that can make or break your success as a person people want to play with. You'll also discover mind games to keep up your spirits as you play. You'll see what equipment you need. Pickleball has two rules: have fun and stay safe. You'll discover ways to warm up your body, so you don't get injured together with advice from coaches and a physical therapist. You'll also learn how to use your body to hit the ball accurately and powerfully.

3. **Get Strategic.** Now that you know the basics, this section will teach you a few simple strategies for beginners, so you aren't merely hitting the ball—you are playing with a purpose. You'll see how to overcome the most common mistakes beginners make.

4. **Get Better.** In this section, you'll see how to find a coach and get the most from a lesson. Plus, you'll find the best drills to improve your game. Not only are they good drills, but they're also fun! You'll find journal pages to chart your progress so you can see how much you are improving week by week.

You can read the book from front to back or in any order you like. You should write in the book, dog-ear the pages, and bring the book with you when you practice or play so you can get the guidance you need when you need it. If you are reading this book on Kindle, you can highlight relevant material.

Why Should I Read a Book When There Are So Many Videos and Articles Online?

Good question.

You've been exposed to so much information in your first lesson or two. You're likely to have forgotten some of what you learned. Or you might be confused as you try to jog your memory. This book puts all the tips, tricks, and techniques you need to know in one place, in a structured way, so you can find what you need quickly and never be baffled again.

Here are a few benefits of reading a physical book compared to watching videos.

1. You can write notes and underline passages so you can make the material your own.

2. You can dog-ear pages so you can find info easily.

3. You can keep track of your progress with the customized journal and assessment sheets I've created for you.

4. You won't have to sift through YouTube videos showing advanced strategies you aren't ready for.

5. You won't have to sit through ads on YouTube videos.

6. You can find info easily instead of having to sit through long videos! Mind you, I love those videos and will refer you to some of the best ones so you can see what to do. However, some videos that should be 30 seconds are fifteen minutes long! You could have played a game of pickleball in that time!

This book does not cover advanced strategies, tournaments, or pro leagues. Since most players will play doubles, we won't discuss the singles game, which is a different—and more demanding—game than doubles.

If you're like most new players who wonder, "How can I play the game without looking like a fool and feeling out of place? How can I meet new people, have fun, and get a bit of exercise without hurting myself?" then this book is for you!

Arnold Palmer said, "Golf is deceptively simple and endlessly complicated; it satisfies the soul and frustrates the intellect. It is at the same time rewarding and maddening—and it is without a doubt the greatest game mankind has ever invented."

He could have been talking about pickleball.

A Brief History

You might have heard about pickleball only recently, but you'd be surprised to know the sport has been played since 1965—nearly half a century.

Three dads created the game to entertain their bored kids on Bainbridge Island near Seattle. Joel Pritchard, Bill Bell, and Barney McCallum looked at a badminton court, lowered the net, and added a hard plastic ball and ping pong paddles. Voilà. A new sport was created.

How the sport got its name is up for debate. Joan Pritchard came up with the name "pickleball" because she enjoyed watching rowing regattas. The non-starters would compete for fun in a "pickle boat" race. Since the new game comprised spare parts, she created the name "pickleball."

An alternative story said their family dog was named "Pickles." However, Pickles was born after the game was created. I guess that creates part of the mystique and folklore that surrounds pickleball.

U.S.A. Pickleball lists the official history on this website:

www.usapickleball.org/what-is-pickleball/history-of-the-game/

The sport was popular in the Pacific Northwest and was taught in schools. Bill Gates learned how to play pickleball! If only he had turned pro in pickleball instead of starting a software company called Microsoft, one can only wonder what the world would be like.

As an homage to its native roots in the Pacific Northwest, the first serve in every pickleball game comes from the northwest service court.

PART 1
Get into the Game

Pickleball takes ten minutes to learn and a lifetime to master.

In this chapter, you'll learn the basics of playing the game with tips from some of America's top pickleball coaches. You'll read their words, see illustrations, and be guided to videos on YouTube so you can fully understand how to play the game properly at a beginner level. You'll learn where to stand, tactics, strategy, and techniques.

There's so much to learn in pickleball, but learning can be easy if you take it one step at a time.

Pam Rauber, a pickleball teacher in northern Georgia said, "I give my students incremental things to work on. And I teach them the rules incrementally."

Chapter 1
Pickleball—The Basics

You might know that pickleball is a paddle sport described as a cross between tennis, ping pong, and badminton. That's because pickleball takes place on a court the size of a badminton court, uses some tennis strokes and terms, and uses ping-pong-like paddles. But the sum of those parts is greater than the whole. Pickleball is better than you would expect from being a combination those individual games.

Pickleball is easier to learn and play than tennis.

According to a CBS News report, just about anyone can pick up the basics and play a game in 30 minutes.

You will pick up pickleball quickly if you have a background in those other racquet sports. My neighbor, Robert, who played tennis for more than 30 years, picked up the sport immediately and started beating other players.

My sport was Scrabble. So, I had a more significant hurdles to overcome! If your sport is watching sports on TV or playing video games, don't worry. You can have fun with pickleball.

However, you can play pickleball on many levels. Pickleball is an easy, fun game where you get exercise and meet people. It can also be a master class in strategy.

"Pickleball is a game of chess with paddles. And the sooner you realize that the better the player you'll become," said Coach Tim.

"I told you, pickleball is a game of strategy."

Let's Cover the Very Beginner Basics

You can play pickleball as singles or doubles. Since most people reading this book will play doubles, that's the game we'll cover. The first team to score eleven points wins the game. They must win by two points.

Only the serving team can score a point. Keeping score is one of the more confusing parts of the game, and you'll see how to demystify scoring in a later chapter.

Pickleball is played with paddles made from various materials, from wood to graphite to polymer. Just don't call the paddle a "racquet." That's a rookie mistake. Racquets have strings.

There is no clock, like in football or basketball. However, games usually take fifteen to 25 minutes to play.

The pickleball is a hard plastic ball with holes. Balls for playing indoors have fewer, larger holes than balls used for outdoor play. You probably won't get hurt if the ball slams into you. Well, getting struck might sting for a second or two, but getting hit by a pickleball is not like a baseball that can cause serious damage. So, don't be afraid of getting hit. However, you should wear eye protection. Balls come in many colors, and you can choose one that fits your style.

Chapter 2
The Lay of the Land

No matter where you play, the size of the court will be the same. Here are the dimensions (which you don't need to know) and the names of the courts and lines (which you must know!)

The court looks like a small tennis court, with an extra horizontal stripe seven feet from the net, called the "kitchen" or the "non-volley zone." If you want to get technical, the court is about one-third the size of a tennis court, which means you don't have to run around as much as in tennis. For all you engineering nerds, the court is 20 wide by 44 feet long, meaning each team's court is only 22 feet long and 20 feet wide. The net is only 36 inches high but droops to 34 inches in the center. Whether you play singles or doubles, you use the entire court, unlike tennis, which uses a smaller court for singles.

COURT DIMENSIONS

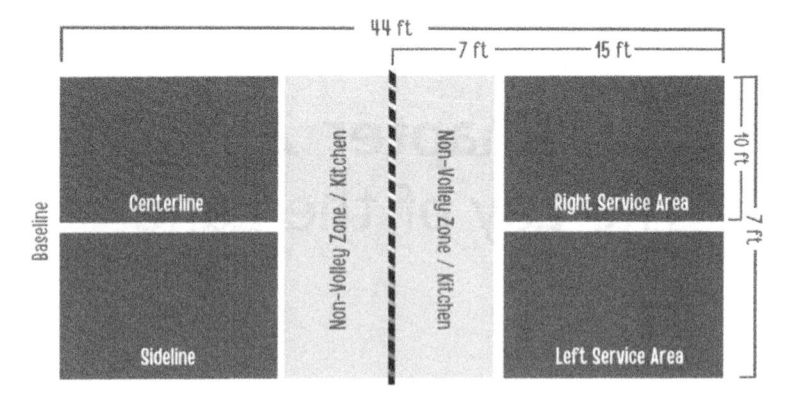

Pickleball court diagram showing: 44 ft total length, 10 ft width, 7 ft non-volley zone from each side of net, 15 ft service area depth. Labeled areas: Baseline, Centerline, Sideline, Non-Volley Zone / Kitchen, Right Service Area, Left Service Area.

Net Height at Sideline is 36 inches
(34 inches at Center)

Notice the court is divided into the right service area and left service area on each side as well as the kitchen, a.k.a. the non-volley zone or NVZ, which extends seven feet from each side of the net. See the rules for the kitchen in the next chapter.

Chapter 3
Two Rules You Absolutely Need to Know

All sports have rules. If you don't follow them, you will lose! Here, you'll learn about two of the more confusing rules: the two-bounce rule and the kitchen rule. In the next chapter, you'll learn the rules for serving which, coincidentally, are also good tips for serving!

Surprisingly, many people don't know the rules—even experienced players! Once a year, the rules committee changes the rules, so be aware of new rules by reviewing this site which contains all the rules:

www.usapickleball.org/what-is-pickleball/official-rules/

Two-Bounce Rule

After the ball is served, the returning team and the serving team must let the ball bounce one time on their side of the net before hitting it. If either team hits the ball out of the air before it bounces on their side at least once, they have committed a fault and that team loses the point.

Kitchen Rules

New players—and some experienced players—don't understand the rules about the kitchen. Let's clear this up once and for all!

- You cannot step into the kitchen to hit a volley (a ball that is hit in the air before it bounces). BUT novice players don't realize you can put your paddle into the kitchen to volley as long as your feet don't go into the kitchen or touch the kitchen line. If you hit a volley but your feet follow through and land in the kitchen, that's a fault and you lose the point. If you hit the ball in the air and your paddle touches the kitchen, it is a fault.

- Here's where people get confused: If the ball bounces into the kitchen, you can step into the kitchen to hit the ball. However, you don't have to wait for the ball to bounce before you enter the kitchen. You just can't hit the ball until the ball bounces.

Watch This!

www.PickleballPublishingCompany.com/KitchenRules

Pro Tip

"If your hips are always square to the net, and you use your upper body to turn, you'll have less chance to land in the kitchen," said Coach M.J. "Less is more. People try to move around too much."

Chapter 4
Terms You Need to Know

Here are words and concepts that will help you understand the game better.

Backhand—A stroke in which you swing the paddle across your body with the back of your hand leading the way.

Bangers—People who hit the ball hard and fast.

Dink A soft shot hit on a bounce from the kitchen into the opposing kitchen.

Drop Shot—A stroke in which the ball bounces harmlessly in your opponent's kitchen, where it cannot be returned as a slam.

Fault—An error that ends a rally, such as hitting the ball out of bounds, hitting the ball into the net, or if the ball bounces twice.

Footwork—Moving your feet to get in the best position to return the ball.

Forehand—A stroke in which you swing the paddle across your body with your palm leading the way.

Kitchen—Also known as the "non-volley zone," the kitchen is the part of the court that extends seven feet from both sides of the net, from sideline to sideline. You cannot step into the kitchen to hit a ball while it is still in the air (a volley). You can step into the kitchen to hit a ball that bounces. You can lean into the kitchen to hit a ball in the air as long as you don't step into the kitchen or touch the kitchen line.

Lob—A ball that goes over the heads of the opponents and lands in bounds.

Pickled—One team shuts out the other. As in, "They beat us. We didn't get a point. We got pickled."

Punch Volley—A stroke in which you punch a volley with a paddle face parallel to the net.

Put Away—A shot that can't be returned.

Rally—Going back and forth over the net multiple times, the play of the ball from the serve until a point or fault occurs.

Side Out—After both players have served and faulted, the other team can serve and score points. On the first serve of the game, side out occurs after the first server's team commits a fault.

Two-Bounce Rule—After the ball is served, the returning team and the serving team must let the ball bounce one time each in their respective courts before hitting it.

Unforced Error—A shot missed because of one's own mistake and not the result of the opponent's skill.

Volley—A ball hit in the air before it bounces.

Winner—A point scored when a ball is hit so well the other team can't lay a paddle on it.

Chapter 5
How to Keep Score

When I asked people on several Facebook pickleball groups what they had the hardest time learning, the number one response was, "How do I keep score? It is so confusing!"

Let's reframe this. Keeping score is not difficult. It is just different! You'll get the hang of it after a few games.

Keeping score in pickleball differs from other sports because two people serve on each possession. Therefore, besides keeping track of the score, we must keep track of which person is serving. Therefore, you need to keep track of three numbers.

"A fun, easy, rhyming method shared with me to help players remember the scoring is:

ME, YOU, WHO," said Coach M.J.

"ME" is your team's score.

"YOU" is the other team's score.

"WHO" is the number of the server.

Before each serve (not during the serve), the server will say her team's score, their opponents' score, and the number of the server.

Here are the likely scenarios:

If your team leads 7-4 and you are the first server, you'd say, "7-4-1."

If your team leads 7-4 and you are the second server, you'd say, "7-4-2."

If your team is behind 7-4 and you are the first server, you'd say, "4-7-1."

If your team is behind 7-4 and you are the second server, you'd say, "4-7-2."

That's not so difficult!

To make things easier, you can say the score and, "I'm server 1."

If your team is leading, 7-4, and you are the first server, you'd say, "7-4, and I'm server 1."

No one will think you are weird if you do this!

If you haven't gotten this committed to memory yet, don't worry. You can always ask your partner for help. We were all beginners at one time! We know what you are feeling.

It isn't uncommon for experienced players to forget the score because they play so many games. They ask their partner or the other team for the score. You won't look out of place.

Scoring sounds more complicated than it is! After you play a few games, scoring will seem natural.

Finally, if the server calls the wrong score, wait until after the rally ends to correct the score.

Scoring Rules

Only the serving team can win a point in pickleball.

You play until one side reaches eleven points. The team must win by two points.

START OF THE GAME

EVEN

EVEN

This team's score will ALWAYS be even when this player is on the right side of the court.

It is easy to lose track of the score! Here's a handy tip. If the serving team's score is even (0, 2, 4, 6, 8, or 10), then the player who was the first server for that team— at the start of the game¬—will be in the right or even court when serving or receiving. If the score is odd, then the first server would be in the left or odd court when serving or receiving.

Chapter 6
Where Do I Stand?

Beginners make a common mistake. "They don't understand the pattern of play," said Coach Charlie. "Servers stay back. Returners run forward."

In a nutshell:

- You go side to side when your team serves and wins a point. After a fault, you stay in the same court.

- When your team receives, one person stands behind the baseline to receive. The other person stands at the kitchen line. After a fault is made, the person at the net goes to the baseline on the same side of the court, while the person at the baseline goes to the kitchen line on the same side of the court. If the serving team faults twice, the receivers are now the servers. The person standing in the right-hand court serves.

● = server

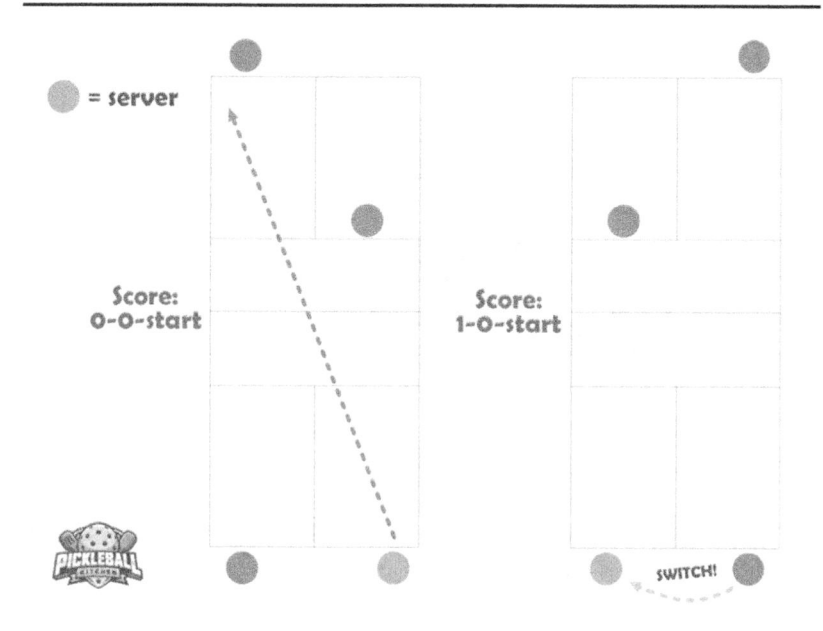

Score:
0-0-start

Score:
1-0-start

SWITCH!

When you're serving, stand behind the baseline. This is a rule. It is also a good practice to stay back after you serve because the returners will want to hit the ball deep. If you run up too soon, the ball will zoom past you.

Remember, positions on the court are not set in stone, and you may need to adjust your position based on where the ball is hit. It's a good idea to practice moving around the court and getting a feel for the different positions. We'll discuss other positionings in relevant sections.

Chapter 7
The Five Stages of a Rally

Now, the fun starts!

Let's look at the five stages of a rally!

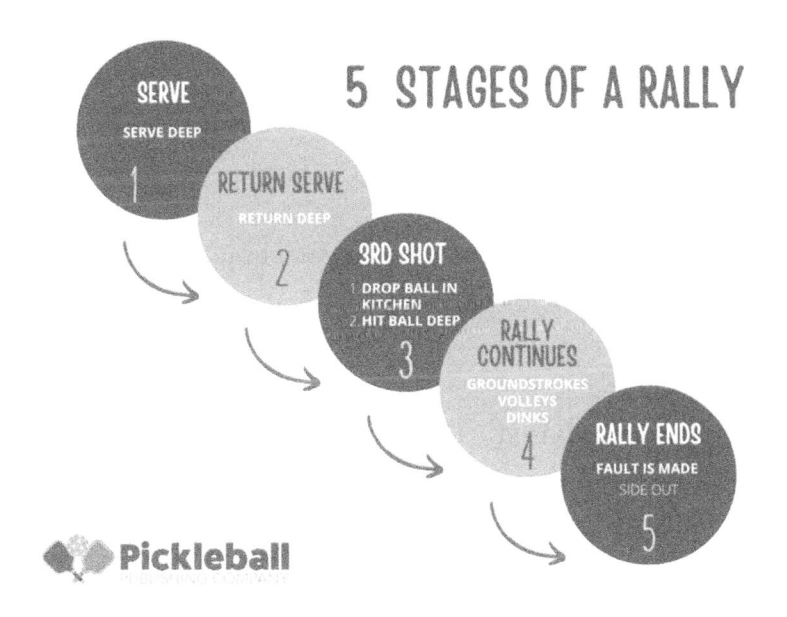

5 STAGES OF A RALLY

1. SERVE — SERVE DEEP
2. RETURN SERVE — RETURN DEEP
3. 3RD SHOT — 1. DROP BALL IN KITCHEN 2. HIT BALL DEEP
4. RALLY CONTINUES — GROUNDSTROKES, VOLLEYS, DINKS
5. RALLY ENDS — FAULT IS MADE, SIDE OUT

Pickleball

How to Serve: Techniques and Rules

As a new player, you will make your partner happy if you consistently serve the ball deep into the correct court. You want to keep your opponents' back near their baseline, so you have an advantage. With a bit of practice, this should be easy!

Coach Tim said, "The biggest thing that holds people back from playing is that they're afraid that if they can't get their serve in. They're embarrassed to play."

Let's help you get over that hurdle!

Let's make this simple. Serving in tennis is hard. Serving in pickleball is easy.

"The most important part about the serve is just to get it in," said Coach M.J. "It doesn't have to be fast."

No partner will ever criticize you if you simply put the ball in play! Unlike tennis, no one expects you to get an ace with your serve.

Coach Clinton advised, "Don't do anything extra with your serve in the beginning. The most important thing is to hit it in and as deep as possible. I always say to new players who try to spin every shot, 'You can bring sexy back later. You can start adding spin and other more advanced elements later.' Just focus on getting the principles down right now."

How do you do that?

The rules and the techniques to serve make this process easy. Fortunately, several rules are actually tips and best practices to help you serve accurately!

Serving Rules

You have to stand behind the baseline. You cannot step into the court. You cannot bounce the ball in the court. You cannot use a side swing or a groundstroke on the serve. Your paddle must contact the ball below your belly button. After you hit the ball, your arm can swing past your belly button.

You get one chance to put the ball into play. There are no "lets" or "double faults" as in tennis. If you fault, the next person serves.

The served ball must land inside the court diagonal from the server. If the ball hits the net and lands in the proper court, the serve is good.

You commit a fault if the ball lands in the wrong court, out of bounds, in your opponents' kitchen, on the kitchen line, or in the net.

If the serving team wins the rally, they score a point. The server and partner switch sides, and the server serves to the receiver in the opposite court.

If the serving team makes a fault, the next person serves. If both servers fault, it is a side out and the other team serves. When the game begins, only the first person on the serving team serves. After that team (both players) faults, the other team serves. This sounds more complicated than it is.

Starting the Game

On the opening serve of the game, only the first player serves. This keeps the play fair. Imagine how lopsided the score could be if both players served before the other team had a chance to serve.

The first server starts serving in the right-hand court, in the northwest position. This is an homage to the game, which started in the Pacific Northwest. The first server serves as long as the team wins points. After that team makes a fault, the other team serves.

Once the second team gets a chance to serve, Server One serves until the team loses a rally. Then Server Two serves until the team loses a rally. Then the other team serves. When both servers have served and made faults, this is called "side out" and the other team can serve.

The next time the first team serves, both players will serve in proper sequence.

Two Ways to Serve

There are two serving styles: a drop serve and a volley serve. In either case, you want to be in a semi-open stance. Imagine you are a batter facing a pitcher in baseball: your feet aren't parallel to the baseline. As you get comfortable serving, you might move to the left or right side of the baseline (never over the centerline!) to get a better angle to deceive your opponents.

The Drop Serve

You can drop the ball at any height. You hit the ball when it bounces up. You must hit the ball below your waist. Remember, the ball will never bounce as high as your waist.

Experiment to find the right height for you. Take ten balls and hit them to imaginary targets near the opposing baseline.

What feels best? Lock that into your muscle memory and you'll have fun getting all your serves in. When you have that technique perfected, aim for different spots so you can target your opponent's backhand and make her guess where you will serve.

Watch This!
www.PickleballPublishingCompany.com/DropServe

The Volley Serve—Forehand Serve

You hold the ball in one hand. You swing your paddle in an upward motion, being careful to hit the ball below your waist. That's a rule.

Watch This!
www.PickleballPublishingCompany.com/ForehandServe

Serving Drills

Visualize This: Muscle Memory for Serving

"Think about cornhole," said Coach Clinton. You know, that simple game based on the bean bag toss.

- Form a solid base.

- Use your shoulder to swing your arm and the paddle.

You might try tossing a ball with your arm in this motion to get the muscle memory locked into your body. You'll be able to see how your arm needs to move to hit the ball deep. Then use a paddle and practice hitting the ball with that same motion and energy.

Serve Strategy

You want to serve the ball deep to keep the other team back. You don't have to have fancy spins or hard shots, as in tennis. Just get the ball over the net. Be aware, more advanced players do put spins on the ball and serve hard and fast. You'll learn to hit those shots and make those serves later.

Return the Serve: The Second Shot

The ball's coming at you!

What do you do?

Don't freak out.

Here's how to return the serve:

- Turn sideways.

- Step in front with your left foot if you're a righty (right foot if you're a lefty).

- Be patient.

- Run to the ball and stop. Don't hit a ball while running. That's a sure way to commit a fault by hitting the ball out of bounds, into the net, or missing it.

- Look at the ball. See the ball contact your paddle.

- Use your torso to generate power.

- Hit the ball deep to keep your opponents pushed back in their court and away from the kitchen.

Coach M.J. said, "A deep return allows you more time to get into position—right up with your partner forming a 'wall at the net' at the kitchen line while making your opponent's third shot more difficult."

Coach Paranto offered this guidance, "Serve deep, return deep. The team that controls the net controls the game."

Watch This! *Return of Serve:*
www.PickleballPublishingCompany.com/ReturnOfServe

A TYPICAL OPENING PICKLEBALL SEQUENCE.

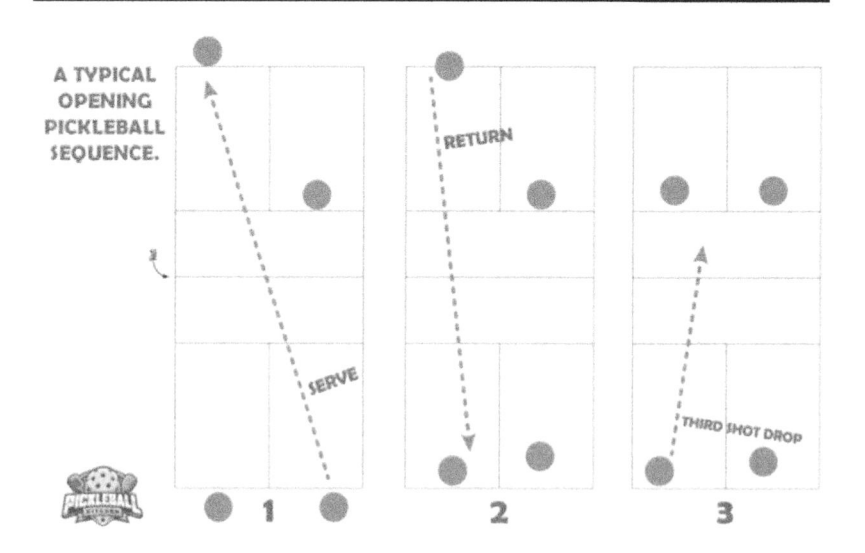

SERVE   1   RETURN   2   THIRD SHOT DROP   3

Third Shot: Two Options

The Serving Team Needs to Earn the Right to Move to the Kitchen

When you are at the kitchen, you are in the best position to return the ball because there are fewer angles the other team can use to get the ball past you.

"You need to capture the kitchen," said Coach Jimbo.

Coach Tim agreed. "If you control the kitchen, you control the game."

If the kitchen is the most important offensive position, how does the serving team get to the kitchen if the other team wants to hit the ball deep? Remember, the servers need to stay back because of the "two-bounce rule," which says the ball must bounce on each side of the court once before you can hit the ball from the air. If you move up too soon, you might hit the ball before it bounces.

When can the serving team safely move up to the net? It depends.

Coach M.J. said, "After you hit the ball, run to the kitchen ONLY IF your return is deep enough! If the return is SHORT and that player immediately charges the net, a good opponent will slam it right past her for the win. The terminology that Professional Pickleball Registry uses is 'mosey' up to the net. It's being able to identify when you've hit a good, NON-ATTACKABLE shot so that you can advance to the kitchen line and still be able to return whatever your opponent hits back. The goal is to advance to the kitchen ASAP, but that needs to be EARNED by hitting a GOOD SHOT."

Most beginners make the mistake of walking into "no-man's-land," a midpoint between the baseline and the kitchen, which can be a dangerous place to stand. You are an easy target for the defenders to attack.

However, Coach Charlie calls this area the "opportunity zone." "It gives you a chance to move up," he said.

"You earn the right to move to the kitchen," said Coach Charlie. "If the defenders hit the ball long, you stay back. If they hit the ball short, you move up." You can hit the ball if they hit it short of the baseline. As they return the ball shorter and shorter, you can move up until you are at the kitchen.

The Third-Shot Drop

And of course, as you perfect your third-shot drop, you will move up.

The third shot is considered the most important one because it can set the tone for the rest of the game. Either the serving team will have an advantage if they play it correctly—or they won't.

You have two options.

If the ball is high or soft, use a groundstroke to hit the ball hard, deep, and down the middle. By trying to hit between the players, you have a chance to confuse them.

However, if the ball is low, use a drop shot, which is a long dink, to place the ball into the kitchen.

Coach Spencer advised, "If you can get the ball to drop in the kitchen, then they have to let the ball bounce. This gives you time to run up to the kitchen. Many people don't understand that you have to loft the ball and have it just land in the kitchen. You can't just take a drive and try to hit softer."

Third-Shot Drop Technique

Hitting a third-shot drop is easier said than done. This is difficult for beginners (or many other players). But that's the goal.

Coach Spencer continued, "When you are returning the drop, be patient. Let the ball drop. After the bounce, let it fall on your paddle instead of hitting it when it is rising. You'll get a better angle if you wait."

Here's a drill to perfect your third-shot drop.

"You need to understand the trajectory of the ball. Stand at the baseline and put your paddle down. Take a ball in your hand and underhand toss it into the kitchen. You'll naturally loft the ball. Once you have an underhand toss that works, pick up a paddle and then try hitting the ball with a paddle."

Here's another tip:

"Let the ball fall onto your paddle," said Coach Paranto.

Watch This!
www.PickleballPublishingCompany.com/ThirdShotDrops

Other Shots

Groundstrokes

Groundstrokes are the basic shots you see in tennis. Stand sideways to the ball, take a compact swing, and move your weight from back to front to increase power and speed. Do NOT take a long backswing. That's common in tennis, but it's a wrong move in pickleball because a long backswing takes too much time and wastes energy.

"When we're hitting ground strokes hard, we're transferring from back to forward. All that adds to consistency," said Coach Paranto. "The closer your head is to the paddle, the more likely you will hit the sweet spot."

Watch This!

www.PickleballPublishingCompany.com/GroundStrokes

Volleys

Volleys are balls hit in the air before bouncing.

Use a short backswing.

Keep your paddle slightly to your backhand.

Reset after each shot.

Watch This!

www.PickleballPublishingCompany.com/VolleyDrill

Punch Volley

You're standing at the kitchen, and the ball comes at you hard and fast.

What do you do?

The punch volley is your best defense.

A punch volley is a short stroke where you push the ball. Aim for your opponent's chest, waist, or feet.

How to hit the punch volley:

- Be in the ready position.
- Hit the ball out in front of you.
- Think of high-fiving the ball.
- Tap the ball. Don't hit it hard.

Watch This!
www.PickleballPublishingCompany.com/PunchVolley

Lobs

Lobs are balls hit in a high arc over the opponent's heads. These shots can thwart the team at the net and force them to run back to hit the ball.

Be careful when you run to hit a lob!

Returning lobs is the way many players get injured.

"If you backpedal, you could fall and hit your head," said Coach M.J. "Don't go backward. You turn and run."

Coach Katie said, "I'll step open and then shuffle back towards the ball. I pretend I'm a catcher in a field. If you know somebody will lob a lot, you can make the plan with your partner and say, 'Hey, Jim is going to be lobbing a lot. I'll run back and get it if it goes over your head. We'll do a switch. That's our plan.'"

Communicate with your partner, so you both don't go for the lob and run into each other!

Because of the difficulty and danger of returning lobs (especially if you are older or have mobility issues), you might decide to not chase the ball.

"There are times when you don't run after the ball and say, 'Hey, man, good shot.' It's not worth killing myself for," said Coach Katie.

Watch This!
www.PickleballPublishingCompany.com/HitALob

Dinks

The dink shot makes pickleball different from other paddle or racquet sports, and it's one of the most fun shots you can make!

While the dink has a funny name, the shot can be devastating.

Here's why. The dink is a soft shot that gently arcs over the net and lands in the opposing kitchen. The closer the ball is to the net, the harder the ball is to hit because of the steep angle you've created.

You can dink in front of your opponents. A cross-court dink makes them run and possibly miss the ball or be out of position to hit your next shot.

"The purpose of a dink is to make your opponents hit the ball up so you can slam the ball back and win the point," said Coach Charlie.

Also, the dink is an excellent way to slow down the game against bangers who hit the ball hard and fast.

Coach Dawson said, "If you hit the ball hard, it will come back hard. If you hit the ball softly, you have more time to prepare. This is old school, classic pickleball. Use the kitchen. The Non-Volley Zone is there for a reason."

Watch This!
www.PickleballPublishingCompany.com/Dinks

The Rally Ends

A fault ends the rally. The next person serves. After both teammates have served and experienced faults, a "side out" occurs and the other team serves.

You play to eleven points and must win by at least two points.

Chapter 8
After-Game Etiquette

After the game ends, all players meet at the net, tap paddles, and say, "Good game."

Pickleball is all about sportsmanship.

Some people touch the handles of their paddles because they think tapping the rims will hurt the paddle. Follow the leader.

If you play at a public court, yell, "Court!" so the next group can come in. If you need to pass through another court to leave the playing area, wait until the other teams have finished their point so you don't disrupt their game.

You can play another game if no one is waiting for your court. Do you want a rematch? Or do you want to mix up the players? Anything goes. Ideally, you'd like the two best players to be on different teams so you can have an evenly paired match.

Congratulations! You've learned the pickleball basics. You know how to get ready to play and how to play the game. Now, you must know how to act so you can fit in nicely and make friends.

PART 2
How to Not Look Like a Newbie

There's no shame in being a new player. However, you want other players to realize you are ready to play. These tips will make you look like you know what you are doing and look like you came for action. Remember the movie *Animal House*? The other characters could spot a freshman a mile away because they wore beanies and acted like dorks. Here are some tips, so you don't look like a dork.

Chapter 9
Getting to Know You: How to Meet Other Newbies

Pickleball is a very welcoming sport. People seem to gravitate toward pickleball as much for the social aspect of meeting new people as they do for exercise or competition. As you go along your pickleball journey, you are bound to meet many kinds of people, just as you would in the rest of the world.

Some people are helpful, kind, outgoing, humorous, and don't take the game too seriously. They want to have fun.

I've played with other people who josh around and have a good time.

I've also met people who want to win at all costs and don't like playing with people who aren't at that same competitive level.

Pickleball doesn't change people. It reveals people.

Some aggressive players will play their top games and use special effects like spinning the ball and hitting bangers to win points against novices—because they want to win. They don't want a "fair fight."

You'll meet so many nice people and a few people are not so nice, just like in real life.

Show people what you want them to see in you.

How to Find "Your People"

I asked people on Facebook forums devoted to pickleball what they wished they had known when they first started playing pickleball. The number one request was, "How do I find people who want to play with me?"

Try these tips to find your people:

1. Join a beginner league at a community center or private club.

2. Find other beginners in classes, clinics, and open play sessions. Make plans to play regularly.

3. Go to a club with open play sessions limited to beginners.

4. Go on Facebook to recruit people. Yes, people do this all the time.

Here Are A Few Ideas to Make New Friends

- Be the first person to reach out and say, "Hi! Wanna play?"

- If you take a lesson or a clinic, get the names and text numbers of the other people in the class and see if they'd like to start a group.

- Ask your pickleball coach if he or she knows other people who'd like to play.

- Enter a tournament at your level so you can meet other people with similar abilities.

Making new friends can be easy.

Don Clements, an avid player, said, "If you move to a new area, pickleball is a great way to meet people. Pickleball is such a social game. If there are four courts, then sixteen people play. But there might be another sixteen people waiting for fifteen minutes or so. I have picked up at least fifteen new friends. I have a whole new group of people I hang around with. On Fridays, we go to a sports bar and drink and have food. When one of us has a birthday, we go to Chicken and Pickle in Overland Park. We rent a few courts and have dinner and drinks."

"Openly admit that you want friends," said Lisa Earle McLeod, author of *Selling with Noble Purpose* and leading authority in emotional engagement. "This is no time to play too-cool-for-school. If you want friends, say so. Out loud. You'll be surprised how many people are actively (but quietly) looking for the same."

To have a friend, be a friend.

She also said, "Model the kinds of relationships you want. Do you want people to ask about your weekend, your kids, or your new affinity for rock climbing? Ask about their lives. Showing genuine interest in other people is the fast track to friendship. It sounds simple. It is simple."

Cathy Paper, a networking coach, a new pickleball player, and a lifelong tennis player, said, "Don't be afraid to ask for advice. We all learn together. If you are not sure of a rule, or how to hit a shot, ask another player or a coach. As new players, we've all been there. That's part of the fun of pickleball. Asking questions connects people."

*"She's getting serious with Richard...
they just signed up for two weeks of pickleball camp."*

No One Can Make You Feel Uncomfortable without Your Consent

Look at Stacie Townsend. She said, "I remember when I was a new player, and I was so intimidated."

She overcame her fears to become the founder of ThePickler.com, a pickleball content and pickleball resource that tries to promote and grow the sport.

Did you feel intimidated? You are not alone!

Coach Barrett Kincheloe said, "One thing I've noticed with complete beginners is that they almost always have a deer-in-the-headlights look."

Coach Barrett continued, "People are almost scared to go out to the courts because it's becoming trendy. It feels like the first day of high school when you go and play for the first time. I tell beginners to focus on friends first. Meet people. Focus on the networking side first. I know that seems crazy, but the thing is that pickleball is so easy to play that you're going to learn the game just fine.

"But finding people and finding friends is one of the essential elements. Because if you go by yourself, you're going to feel like you're not going to fit in. People may not notice you. They may not want to take the time to come over and show you the ropes. But if you go with someone, you have a little bit more confidence. Find someone to connect with in some way. It will make that first week so much easier. I remember how it felt to be a beginner. It's not fun feeling like you're the only person on the court that has no idea what's going on.

"But remember this. There are tens of thousands of people out there in your shoes as well. You're not the only one! Your first time out on the court might be a bit awkward, but that's okay! Most open-play locations will be just fine with having complete beginners there. In fact, some open-play locations are designed for beginners. Don't be afraid to reach out to the coordinators and ask them about it. The vast majority of pickleball players and coordinators want more beginners at their locations."

Coach Dawson said, "Don't be bashful. The pickleball community is friendly." People say:

- "Hey, do you want to play?"
- "Do you want to learn?"
- "Can I help you?"

"Everyone is so friendly. All questions are answered nicely. Those are the kind of people who play pickleball to begin with," said Coach Dawson, whose motto at Bobby Riggs Racquet and Paddle is, "Be Kind. It Matters."

Starting a Conversation

How can you get to know people?

Shy people have a difficult time starting conversations. I've found one way that works is to become an object of interest. Give the other people who are outgoing something to start a conversation with. For example, wear a t-shirt with a favorite vacation destination, like the Grand Canyon or a ski area. That's likely to start a conversation. Or wear a sports team logo shirt or hat. People will ask, "Are you from...?" Extroverts love to talk. They just need an "in" to get started. Help them out, and you'll make a new friend.

Don't talk about money, religion, politics, or sex at the first few meetings.

Use Technology to Set Up Your Games

Once you find several people who want to play together, get organized. Use the *TeamReach* app to let people know when the next game is and who can come. The app is free at the App Store on your iPhone. I found dozens, if not hundreds, of pickleball groups that use this app. Of course, you can set up an e-mail list or a phone list with your friends.

Chapter 10
I Want to Play with YOU! Be a Good Pickleball Partner

You and your partner are a team. You win together. You lose together. You have fun together.

Or you get on each other's nerves!

No one will mind playing with a new player if you are a good partner. Fortunately, you can become popular by following these simple steps. Here are ways to win friends and influence your positive playing.

1. Introduce yourself. Be the first person to say, "Hello. My name is..."

2. No one remembers names! If you played with someone before but didn't remember their name, don't be afraid to ask again. "Gee, I'm bad with names. What did you say your name was?"

3. Let your partner know you are new or have been playing for only a few months. She'll help you.

4. Tell your partner about your strengths or weaknesses, such as, "My backhand sucks," "I'm a good dinker," or "I have a bad knee, so I can't run for the ball."

5. During the game, communicate clearly with your partner. Let her know if you are going to take a shot that is near both of you. Many balls down the middle go unhit because each person thinks the other will take the shot. "Use as few words as possible. Say, 'mine,' or 'yours.' It doesn't have to be 'I've got it.' There's too much language," said Coach Jimbo. You can yell, "Let it go," if you think the ball will fly out of bounds. You might have a better view than your partner, so this call can help you win a point.

6. Move with your partner. "I like to think of hitting in pickleball much like an accordion. You go up together. You come back together. The applicable word is together," Coach Jimbo said. If you run to the sideline to return a shot, your partner should move closer to you to cover the area you left vacant. That's where your opponent will want to hit the ball.

7. Respect your partner. He might be having a lousy day. Do not give comments like, "You should have done this or that."

8. Congratulate your partner and your opponents when they make a good shot. Call out, "Good shot," "Good get," or "Nice serve." People like compliments.

9. If they mess up, as we all do, offer encouragement. "Good try!"

10. Never criticize, condemn, or complain.

11. Some people tap each other's paddles lightly after making a good shot. However, some people think tapping paddles will ruin the edges. They tap their handles instead. Follow your partner's lead.

12. At the end of the game, all players meet at the net and say, "Good game," or "Thank you," and tap their paddles. Some people touch the rims of their paddles while others touch the handles.

13. If you are not ready for the other players' level of competition, thank everyone for the game and move on to another court where you can play against other people closer to your abilities.

When you are a good sport and have a good attitude, your partner will forgive you for missing a shot.

*"Dad, just for today, can everything **not** be about pickleball?"*

Meet a Pickleball Ambassador

U.S.A. Pickleball, the governing body of Pickleball in the United States, created the Ambassador Program to promote pickleball in local areas. These volunteers work with the communities, clubs, and other recreational facilities to guide and help build pickleball programs for all to enjoy.

For more information on how you can become an ambassador, go to: www.usapickleball.org/get-involved/usa-pickleball-ambassadors/

Dan: Why did you want to become a Pickleball Ambassador?

Lydia Hirt: I joined to become an ambassador to give the sport I love a little legitimacy, hopefully spread the word and help other people discover how to get involved with pickleball in the greater New York City area.

I was motivated to do this because pickleball in New York City is unofficial and more of a pop-up community. It's hard to figure out how to get involved.

Dan: What challenges do you see?

Lydia: The [pickleball] community is great. I think the frustrations often stem from there being significantly more demand to play here in NYC than there is availability and access. I am hoping for more permanent courts and potentially indoor locations since we have all four seasons.

It's less of a frustration with other players and more the lack of infrastructure. We have to support the interest in pickleball.

People bring their own nets. People are waiting. So, we're doing four on, four off. You're getting into a game with a random group of people, which is a beautiful way to meet new people who become friends. Though waiting between games and the mix of levels on the court can be frustrating, which sometimes leaves beginners and experienced players feeling frustrated.

We want to keep everybody happy, but the court I most often play on is an open playground. You'll have a relatively intense pickleball game going on with all this other stuff happening. We have football players. We have kids doing science projects. We have kids skateboarding through the court. It's wild. You just kind of have to accept it as a New York experience and hopefully feel a sense of charm.

Dan: What do you do in your role as a Pickleball Ambassador?

Lydia: I field a lot of questions from people looking to get involved.

Dan: What is your biggest accomplishment as an ambassador?

Lydia: In my role as ambassador and on my social media, I focus on building a community centered around people who also love pickleball.

Dan: How can other people create a community? What tips do you have for them?

Lydia: Be open, be friendly, and help people connect with other players at their level. When I'm traveling to a new place, I will often seek out a community online before arrival to see if I can set up any games in advance. And I'm always willing to speak with strangers playing on a court or who are carrying pickleball paddles.

People should be kind, considerate, and respectful.

Dan: What do you like most about pickleball?

Lydia: I've made hundreds—literally hundreds—of friends in the year and a half I've been playing pickleball. It's been really special. The community is my favorite part of pickleball. These are people of all ages and all demographics who I likely would not have met otherwise.

When I go upstate, two of my closest friends are retired and decades older than me, and I genuinely enjoy playing with them. I bring my paddle with me on every trip and always try to find a pickup game in the local community. I've found pickleball to be a powerful way to connect with different destinations and people.

Dan: How often do you play?

Lydia: As much as possible. I played this morning before the workday started. It's better than coffee for me and I find I'm in a much better mood when I play before opening my laptop!

Dan: How can newbies fit in?

Lydia: We have a lot of new people coming, and I do always recommend that they familiarize themselves with the basic rules of the game.

Nobody is expecting you to be a beast at the net right away, but you should have that basic understanding of the point-scoring system, the goals of the game, and how to be a good partner.

Be friendly. Be a good sport. Acknowledge that you're new and try to connect with other beginner players.

Watch the community for a little bit and see how people are playing before you put your paddle down [to reserve your spot in a game]. Learn the rotation to wait for courts. Be positive, smile, and laugh. It's called pickleball, after all. So try not to take yourself or anybody else too seriously.

Check out Lydia's social media:

- Instagram:
  www.instagram.com/lydia.pickleball/

- Newsletter, "Love At First Dink":
  loveatfirstdink.substack.com

- Email: lydia.pickleball@gmail.com

- LinkedIn: www.linkedin.com/in/lydiahirt/

Chapter 11
Dress for Success: What Equipment Do I Need?

Few sports require as little equipment as pickleball. Of course, you need to buy a paddle and pickleballs. You probably have everything else you could need: comfortable clothes, sneakers, suntan lotion, a hat or visor, possibly a sweatband, and a towel. You will want to bring a water bottle to hydrate before, during, and after each game.

You might want to wear safety glasses and elbow or knee braces. Don't forget sunglasses and a hat with a visor to block the glare on sunny days.

Don't Call It a "Racquet:" How to Select a Paddle

Pickleball paddles come in all shapes, sizes, colors, and materials. Price ranges from about $35 to over $200.

Avoid lower-quality paddles. They could cause you to develop tennis elbow. New technologies have helped create exceptionally smooth and powerful paddles. Look for neoprene paddles with a honeycomb interior design to absorb shock. They reduce vibration and impact. Your body will thank you.

I use the PROKENNEX Pro Flight Pickleball Paddle. That's also the paddle Coach Tim chose after doing a blind test of 40 paddles. http://www.PickleballPublishingCompany.com/products

Everyone is different, and every paddle is different. Try a few. You can borrow paddles at a club or your local pickleball store.

Paddle Test

1. Does it feel comfortable?

2. Does it absorb shock, or does your arm reverberate each time you hit the ball?

3. Do you feel pain in your hand, shoulder, elbow, or wrist using the paddle—or 24 hours later?

4. Does the grip feel comfortable?

Balls

Nearly every pickleball game starts with someone asking, "Who has a ball?"

I think that's incredibly cheap and shows you are ill-prepared.

Be the person who says, "I have a ball."

Pickleball uses two types of balls optimized for indoor or outdoor play. Indoor balls have 26 larger holes. Outdoor balls have 40 smaller holes. Be sure to buy the right ball for the right court. Balls come in several colors: yellow, blue, green, orange, and pink. You can choose any color you like.

Please note, some indoor courts could have outdoor surfaces! Use outdoor balls even though you are playing inside.

You can buy pickleballs for about $3 a ball at many sporting goods stores and pickleball clubs.

Outdoor balls (left) have smaller holes.
Indoor balls (right) have larger holes.

Shoes

All shoes are not created equal.

"Tennis shoes or running shoes don't offer any lateral stability often have too much grip. So we see a lot of Achilles or ankle injuries," said Nate Stier, co-owner of OSR Physical Therapy with offices in suburban Minneapolis, www.osrpt.com.

He advises people to wear "court shoes," noting that "tennis shoes" have come to mean just about any kind of sneaker.

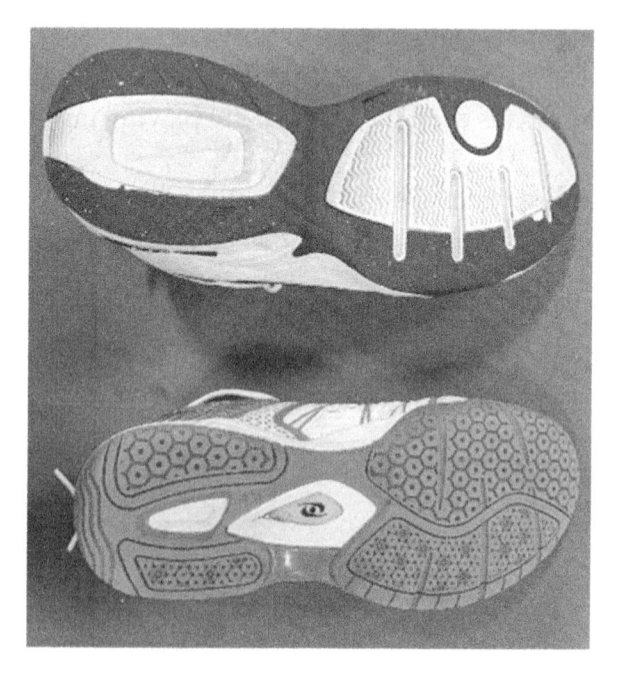

Court shoes named "Dink Shot" from Acacia (bottom) provide the support needed for pickleball. Running shoes (top) do not.

"Running shoes go forward, not sideways. People sprain their ankles or break an ankle because they're shuffling sideways, but those shoes are not made to go that way," he said. "This leads athletes to roll their ankles and fall. This can result in ankle sprains along with upper body injuries from the fall, such as hand/wrist fractures and concussions. Pickleball requires a lot of quick lateral movement. If athletes are wearing running shoes that don't offer the support needed, it can lead to ankle sprains and other injuries due to falling. Shoe choice is very important in reducing the chance of injury."

Coach Paranto agreed. "If you don't wear the right shoes, you could end up with a wrist fracture. We've seen a few people with twisted ankles from falling, or we've seen fractured wrists from putting their hands out to catch themselves when they fall."

You might also want to add sport insole inserts in your shoes to provide support.

Bags

You'll want to use a bag to carry your equipment, keys, wallet, phone, and other personal supplies. You could buy a bag designed for pickleball, but any backpack will do. Most people don't care about fashion. But feel free to express yourself in your clothing if it makes you more confident.

Pro Tip

Carabiners - You probably never heard of a carabiner unless you are a mountain climber. Simply put, they are large hooks that look cool. You'll want to buy a carabiner to hang your bag on the fence to protect your valuables from puddles or someone stepping on your bag. The carabiner will show everyone you know what you are doing. And isn't looking good 90% of any activity?

Pickleball bags hang safely on a fence thanks to carabiners.

SUPPLY LIST

- [ ] Backpack
- [ ] Water bottle
- [ ] Lunch
- [ ] Snacks
- [ ] Pen
- [ ] Caribiner
- [ ] Phone
- [ ] Keys
- [ ] Suntan Lotion
- [ ] Court Shoes

- [ ] Paddle
- [ ] Balls
- [ ] Hat or sun visor
- [ ] Sweat towel
- [ ] Business cards
- [ ] Eye Protection
- [ ] Membership Card
- [ ] Bug spray
- [ ] Sun glasses

Pickleball
PUBLISHING COMPANY

Chapter 12
Where Can I Play, and What Should I Pay?

Pickleball courts are popping up all over the world!

You will find public courts in parks, schools, rec centers—even some churches! You'll find private courts at clubs, apartment complexes, and fitness centers.

If you are a senior, check if your community center or gym accepts Silver Sneakers. You might play for free! Some courts might have special hours only for seniors or for leagues.

You will see more and more facilities adding pickleball courts. New national and regional pickleball chains are getting into the action. And don't forget the new kind of restaurant that has pickleball courts, bars, and lounges.

You can find a court near you simply by going to Google and typing, "Where can I play pickleball near me?" You'll find lots of links!

Yes, there's even an app for that. *Places2Play and Pickleheads* both lists courts all over the U.S. with addresses, hours, fees, directions, and—get this—ratings for friendliness, wait times, variety of play, and the facility. Yes, the apps are free at the App Store on your iPhone.

You can also search Facebook for pickleball groups in your community. You can ask members where they play, the culture, and the fees.

Private clubs and restaurants charge whatever the market will bear—anything from a few dollars to $35-50 per hour! They also might charge an initiation fee. You'll find nationwide fitness centers, like Life Time, have embraced pickleball and have different rates for different levels of membership or for different times of the day based on demand.

You might find that each court has its reputation. Some are welcoming and friendly. Some attract advanced or aggressive players. Some have hours for seniors, tennis players, or leagues.

That's okay. Finding the court that is best for you is always better. I found beautiful courts in Staring Lake in Eden Prairie, Minnesota. On a beautiful Saturday morning, the courts were packed. Paddles filled all the slots in the paddle rack. I hadn't seen a paddle rack before, so I asked a friendly-looking guy what the procedure was.

He realized I was a newbie. He said—in the nicest, kindest way possible—that I would be better off if I went to courts in

Hopkins, a nearby city! He implied I'd get killed on these courts, and I would have a better experience at the other site. I took this as a positive message. I went to the courts in Hopkins, and I had a very good time! I became friends with many people there and played with them frequently.

You'll want to find a place that welcomes and encourages newbies. You want to avoid courts that are overly aggressive and competitive. It's no fun playing against people who are much better than you are, especially when you are a beginner.

The Best Time to Play

Every court is different, of course, but here are several scenarios you are likely to see:

1. Public courts in the middle of the day are usually nearly empty. You can play with your partners in a relaxed atmosphere for as long as you like unless other people are waiting.

2. Public courts could be packed in the early morning and right after normal work hours.

3. You can reserve courts at clubs for a fee. You can play whenever you want, provided the court has an opening. Some private clubs will have open play hours for people at each competition level, so you can play against people who are at your level. They also might have leagues, so you can play with people at your level.

Playing Indoors and Outdoors

What could be better than spending an hour outdoors, soaking up the sun, feeling the wind in your hair, and smelling the freshly cut grass at an outdoor pickleball park?

Or you might say, what could be worse than ruining your hair, sneezing from allergies, and getting lobster red from a sunburn? If that sounds like you, an indoor court is in your future!

If you play outside, the weather can be a factor. A gust of wind could rocket your ball out of bounds—even if you merely tapped it! Your powerful serve could go short if the wind is blowing against you. A ball you are about to slam could take a left-hand turn as the wind hits it. When you warm up, take the measure of the wind, and adjust your strokes as needed.

The bright sun can temporarily blind you. A good hat can block some or all of the sun. However, you can ask to switch sides after one team has scored six points, so the weather affects everyone equally.

If it rains, the court will be wet and unplayable. Don't risk an injury by playing on a court that is wet or only partially dry.

Some courts are well maintained, while others might show signs of wear and tear. Notice any cracks that might trip you.

How many games have been canceled because the weather was too hot, too muggy, too windy, too cold, or even too snowy? That's why some people like to play indoors. Of course, in cold-weather cities, outdoor courts will be closed for the winter. You'll need to find a place to play indoors.

When you play indoors, you don't have to worry about the sun or wind. However, some indoor courts have their peculiarities.

Many indoor pickleball courts, especially in community centers and mixed-use facilities, share space with basketball courts and tennis courts. Each sport marks its boundaries with different colored lines. You simply need to see which colored line applies to pickleball. You might need a few minutes to adjust to the rainbow of colors.

Two pickleball courts with nets are set up inside a basketball court. Watch out for the hoops!

If you play indoors at a mixed-use basketball court, you might have to contend with a basketball backboard and hoop that hangs over the pickleball court and could interfere with high shots.

Going Clubbing?

Joining a club has several advantages over going to a public court. You can reserve your time, so you know you will have a court to play on. Clubs also offer lessons and drills so you can improve your game. They also might feature leagues and open play so you can find people to play with. Those facilities might also have different times set aside for different level players, so you know you will play with people at your level, which means you will have the most fun.

Coach Katie said, "The advantage of going to a club like Life Time is that you have staff who can guide you through your experience. We create different opportunities for people of different levels. We have open play for beginners and general open play for all levels. There are times for anyone at any level to come in and mix in and have that authentic pickleball experience. We are trying to create niches for people to play against the competition they want. But we still have open play pickleball for all levels. So, when you go to a club, it's like going to a buffet. You can choose the days, times, and activities that you want to be involved with. It's like a one-stop shop for everything that you might want. There is camaraderie at a club. They all have the commonality of belonging to the club, so they have things in common. They make friends. They see each other. They go out to eat."

Clubs could offer other entertainment options.

Coach Katie also said, "We have a bar and a Life Café. So, there are healthy options. I think that'll be a nice place for people to socialize. It's another built-in experience for people to enjoy. They don't have to figure it all out. They can just come in and have their full pickleball experience. It's kind of like being on a cruise ship. You know, just go, and you can stay all day. You can work out. You can eat, drink, and play pickleball. What else do you need?"

Chapter 13
How to Get into a Game: Open Play for Everyone!

Open play is the time when anyone can come to a court and play with anyone else. Chances are this will be your go-to activity unless you play with a group of friends. There's a special vibe and a set of rules to open play. Let's dig in so you feel like one of the gang.

You've arrived at a court. All the courts are full. People are sitting on picnic tables or stadium benches. Everyone seems to be having a good time.

Here's how you can get into a game and start making new friends.

It's not uncommon to see 30, 40, or 50 people on a public court on a Saturday morning. So how do you determine who will play next? Public courts usually have a "first-come, first-served" rule. There are no reservations. Unlike tennis, where people reserve a court for an hour, public pickleball courts rotate the players, so everyone gets a chance to play without waiting forever.

Every court or club has its own rules, but these rules seem to be universal.

Many courts use a long paddle rack with slots to hold 16 or 32 paddles. Players put their paddles into the rack in the order they arrive. They meld or rotate into games as courts open. The red, white, blue, green, and yellow banners mark the next groups of players.

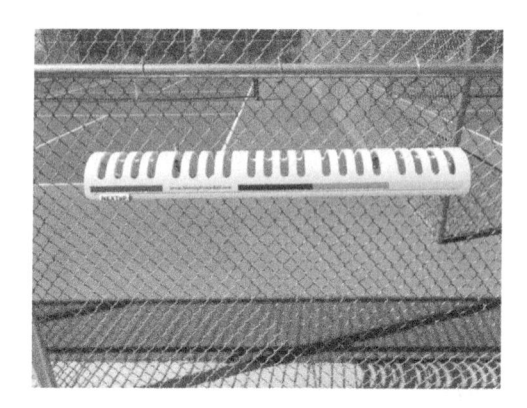

The "Next Up!" marker shows who will play next.

In this picture, the first four slots atop the red banner are empty, which means those players who were next in line picked up their paddles and headed to their court. And they moved the "Next Up" button to the next group of paddles, which are atop the white banner. When new people arrive, they will put their paddles into the empty slots.

Each court has its rules, but I've found many courts use this system to ensure everyone gets a chance to play often without waiting too long to get into a game.

1. If nine paddles are in the rack, all four players must leave the court after the game ends. The next four paddles on the rack take the court.

2. If fewer than nine paddles are in the rack, the losing team leaves, and the following two players in the rack rotate into the empty spots on court.

3. Players who want to play together can keep their paddles together and wait for the appropriate number of slots to open.

4. If four players leave the court and put their paddles into the rack, the winning team's paddles go in first so they can play before the losing team.

If you want to play with a friend, spouse, or partner, you can put your paddles together and wait for a chance to play together.

You can pass up your turn if you are tired and need to rest, or if you will be paired with people you'd rather not play with (like really, really good players who don't enjoy playing with newbies, or people who hit the ball so hard, you can't even see the ball). No one will be offended.

Pro Tip

Because many paddles look alike, write your name on your paddle near the handle. I put a green rubber band on the handle, so my paddle stands out from similar paddles.

Get in the Game

You've put your paddle into the rack, and your turn is ready! What do you do next?

One of the more outgoing players might grab the next four paddles and raise them to the air so people can see who is in the next game. Take your paddle and introduce yourself to your new friends.

Pick teams. Let everyone know you are new. The best player should play with the newest player to keep the game fair. Of course, anyone can play with anyone.

Before your first game, you should warm up. Warming up in pickleball means hitting a few dinks with someone on the other team. Let the other players know you'd like to warm up. They will gladly accommodate you. You can also use the warm-up period to practice a few longer shots and serves. Let people know when you are ready to play.

You should always use two balls to warm up. That way, each person gets more practice.

Take mental notes of the wind and sun to see if they will factor into your play. After a minute or two, someone will say, "Is everyone ready?" Or "Are you ready?" And you'll begin your first game.

Now you are ready to play!

Being nervous is natural. But don't be scared!

Chapter 14
Playing at Your Level

If you want to have fun, play with people at your level.

Coach M.J. said, "People like to play with people at their level. Finding people at your level is less intimidating and more welcoming. You get better when you play with people at your level. If you don't have the basics, then playing against better players will not help you."

"Of course," she continued, "some people are natural athletes, and they can pick up things. If you are a better athlete, then you can play against better opponents."

All is good if you play with friends or join a clinic or league with people with similar abilities.

But what happens when you go to an open play or public court where people of all abilities play, and you join their games?

Some people will play with you. They realize they need to "pay it forward" because others helped them in the beginning. Other people are jerks. Let's discuss this, so you can make friends with better players.

Should Newbies Play with Experienced Players? The Case for Playing with Better Players

Playing with people at your level is more fun. The rallies are longer. You can practice more shots. You will win more games. When you play with slightly better people, you will see different shots, like spins and well-placed balls. You will get incrementally better. However, if you play against people who are much better, you will get your head handed to you on a platter. That experience is not fun!

When you play with people at your level, you can use all the shots you learned in your lessons or online. You'll win some. You'll lose some. And you'll have fun playing. I heard a major league ballplayer say in an interview, "You don't have time to experiment in the big leagues." I think this same rule holds true when you play against people who have superior skills.

"A completely new player should not be playing with people who are better than you because you're just going to get frustrated, and you're just going to burn out immediately," said Coach Barrett. "Playing better players happens once you get into the improving stage of pickleball, but not in the beginning stages."

Coach Barrett also said, "You want consistency early on. You're playing with people who you enjoy being around. That will let the addiction sink in. And with that experience, you'll ask, 'What can I do better?' That's when you should start playing people who are better than you. Focus on that fun part of it. Focus on that social aspect."

Open Play: When You Play with Players of Every Level

When you play in "open play," you might play against much better players. That's okay. The general ethos is that experienced players will play with new players and be good sports. But that's not always the case.

Some people come for social play and don't care if they win or lose.

Other people seek a competitive game where they can test themselves and improve.

Pickleball can be played on many levels. If all you want to do is go out to the court with a bunch of friends and hit the ball with some friends, that's fine.

Some people play four or five times a week—or more—against the same people. They become friends. When you come to the court, some people will be receptive to new players and others will not. But one thing is sure: they are all good. After all, they play ALL THE TIME. Here are a few ideas on how to fit in.

How do better players feel about playing against new players?

Coach Spencer said, "It depends. I would like to think most players are happy when they see beginners and that new people are getting into the sport. We're still in that phase. When you tell people you are new, they will be cool with it. Everyone who plays pickleball wants to see the sport grow."

But don't take advantage of their kindness.

"Thank [the more experienced players] for playing with you. They are respecting you by playing with you. Respect them by not hogging their time. You don't want to be labeled as 'that guy.' Etiquette goes both ways. I can always practice something even if I'm playing someone at a lower level."

Coach Katie said, "People who are better players should be kind, courteous, and welcoming. They should play with people who are beginners. You should let them know you are a beginner player right off the bat. When I started, I took a lot of advice from people. I think you should be open to advice from other people. They're just trying to help. It's a really good way to learn the game. You don't have to follow everything, but it's good to try it out, anyway. Don't expect to play in all the games. Bow out after two games if it's not the right fit for you."

Some people like to play for fun, friends, and exercise. Others are ultra-competitive and play in tournaments.

Eve Fields, a retired attorney who plays in New Jersey and Florida, said, "I think there is another group (like me). Some people like to have a good, competitive game and might feel disappointed if the others on the court don't provide that. Still, they will never insult other people or make another player feel bad. On the contrary, they will compliment the good shots and give positive advice if the partner is receptive. Players at a lesser level know it and probably self-assess. So positive, friendly advice is typically welcomed. Nobody plays better when she feels as if her partner is sneering under her breath.

"I think the welcoming factor in pickleball is very simple, as it is in many sports (though it doesn't necessarily work in all sports). I call it the 'play it forward' method. Somebody had to be nice to me at one point to welcome me. I try to do the same thing when I see a newcomer. It's easy in golf because the 'not as good' player can just move the ball forward or pick up her ball. But it's more difficult just to do that in pickleball or tennis. I am sure each facility has different times for different levels to play. It's when someone thinks they are SO MUCH BETTER than almost anybody else that a problem arises."

Tips for Starting with an Experienced Partner

"I would always ask questions first. Be the first person to be curious. I think curiosity helps with ego and etiquette," said Coach Barrett. "Ask them, 'Hey, how long have you been playing for?' They'll say, 'Oh, six months,' or whatever. You can say, 'Oh, wow, that's cool,' to get their ego going in the right direction. And then you can say, 'Okay, great. I'm brand new. And I would love to learn something from you if you do that.' That is an easy way for them to feel they have to give back in a way because you complimented them."

Fear and Loathing on the Pickleball Court

Remember the "Mean Girls" from high school? They play pickleball now!

Most pickleball players are friendly people who want to meet other people and have a fun time. However, pickleball snobs will want to play only with people at their level. That's okay, but some people are simply rude about doing this!

One woman I know moves the paddles of waiting players so she will not have to play with certain people! One person told me, "Even her husband doesn't like to play with her."

You can't make this up!

Other people are plain insensitive. One person told me he was playing at a community center when one person told another player with a physical limitation, "You don't belong here." Remember, this was at a public facility with open play. That negative person was probably a jerk in real life and brings his bad vibes to the pickleball court and everywhere else.

Footnote to the story: the newer player called the community center's director and told her the story. She banned that rude player! Karma!

Remember: You have the right to be on a court. Everyone has the right to play.

Chapter 15
The Pickleball Code: Unwritten Rules for Success

Remember the classic line in the movie *A League of Their Own* when Tom Hanks said, "There is no crying in baseball!"

Every sport has rules and "unwritten rules." In baseball, the rule is three strikes, and you are out. No debate. An unwritten rule is, "You don't bunt to get a hit in the ninth inning when your team is leading 10-0. If you do, you'll get a fastball thrown at your butt on your next time at bat!"

Pickleball has unwritten rules too. Fortunately, you won't get hit in the butt if you don't follow them. The rules are easy to follow. You'll win brownie points when you do!

1. No cursing. If you miss a shot, don't drop an F-bomb. Everyone misses shots. Easy shots. Hard shots. Impossible shots. Keep your thoughts to yourself.

2. Don't say "I'm sorry." We'd like to apologize to our partner for missing an easy shot or messing up a serve, but you don't need to say, "Sorry." If everyone said, "Sorry," after every bad play, you'd hear nothing but "I'm sorry" all day long.

3. No trash talk such as insulting comments meant to demoralize, intimidate, or humiliate someone. This is common in basketball but disdained in pickleball.

4. Don't give advice in pickleball unless someone asks. Giving unsolicited advice is considered rude and condescending. If you are new and want advice, let your partner know. He or she might appreciate your willingness to learn. But beware. "Over 70 percent of advice is wrong. You should always rely on the advice you received from a trusted coach. Or go online and study a video from a high-level player," said Coach Tim.

5. If your ball goes on another court, yell "ball" or "ball on court" so those people don't trip over your ball.

6. If a ball from another game lands on your court, stop playing, toss the ball to the other players, and repeat the point.

7. When you must pass another court to get to your court or return to the waiting area, wait for a pause in their game. Otherwise, you will distract those players.

8. At open play, when you are matched with three strangers, let them know you are a newer player.

9. At open play, create teams where the two best players are on opposite sides. Please note some "teams" will refuse to break up. Oh well. I guess that's an unwritten rule to an unwritten rule!

10. On the serve, the person positioned at the kitchen on the returning team should stand sideways to get a good look at the serve to determine if the ball is in or out. If it is out, shout "out" loudly! If it is good, say nothing and take your position at the kitchen line.

If you follow these guidelines, most people will want to play with you.

"I told you, Mike. Pickleball means never having to say you're sorry."

Pickleball Does Have Real Rules Too!

You can't play any game until you know the rules. Fortunately, you don't have to read the entire rule book to play and have fun. You need to know the rules related to sportsmanship and gameplay to get started. I'll slowly dribble out other rules at the appropriate times, so you don't get overwhelmed with dos and don'ts.

1. The receiving team calls the balls in or out. Yell "short" if the ball lands in the kitchen, "wide" if it lands on the wrong side of the line, or "out" or "long" if it lands outside the court. If there is any doubt about whether the ball is out or in, the call is made in favor of the opponent. Pickleball is all about fair play. If you can't decide if the ball is in or out and you hit it — but your partner calls the ball out — then the ball is out. When playing with friends, you might decide to do a "do-over" if there is a disagreement.

2. If there's too much wind or sun, either side can ask to switch sides after one team has scored six points. That way, neither team has an advantage because of the weather.

3. If you are the receiver standing at the net, you need to be aware of two problems. If the served ball hits you, or if you catch the ball, you have committed a fault (an error that ends a rally) and the other side gets the point! You must get out of the way. Usually, this results from a bad

serve, but some nasty players aim the ball at the net person if the player at the net isn't paying attention.

4. If you hit a ball that is called out, the ball is dead. Sometimes our bodies work faster than our minds or mouths, so we hit first and think later. Or we can't tell if the ball is in or out.

5. However, if the ball hits you on a fly while you stand out of bounds, it is a fault.

For a complete list of rules, go to: www.usapickleball.org/what-is-pickleball/official-rules/

"Yeah, I call that out of bounds."

Here's a sign I saw in a community center:

> ## In the spirit of pickleball:
>
> 1. Be respectful and inclusive of players at all levels and ages.
> 2. Recreational players should look to play with similarly skilled players.
> 3. Upper-level players should be available to play a game with lower skill levels.
> 4. Players who are not welcoming will be asked to leave.

There Ought to Be a Rule!

Enter tournaments at your level! Some advanced players (I won't mention names, but you know who you are) enter tournaments for beginners and lower-ranked players.

Why?

So they can win a trophy.

That's like registering your fifteen-year-old kid to play in the league for ten-year-olds.

Do players like that deserve that trophy?

I think not.

Let tournament directors know if those players are "cheating."

And for the tournament directors reading this book, please make sure that people sign up for their appropriate skill levels so we can all have fun.

Chapter 16
Mind Games: Keep a Positive Attitude

Your attitude could be a critical factor in your enjoyment of pickleball. If you beat yourself up after you miss an easy shot, or if you hang your head after you lose three games in a row, you will not have any fun.

Be careful how you talk to yourself. Be mindful of your inner dialog. Avoid self-deprecating dialog.

Don't beat yourself up by talking negatively to yourself if—and when—you miss a shot.

"They say you become what you think about all day long. Right? I never think, 'I'm getting old.' I'm just glad I'm getting older," said Coach Tim.

Norm Brekke, a retired Army officer, has two rules for people who play in his group: have fun and don't get hurt!

If you have a positive attitude like that, you can't lose!

If you think winning is the only way to measure your success, I'll invite you to use my "reframe" of what winning means: "If I improve one skill, or meet one new person, then I've won."

Robert, a Gen-X Realtor said, "I don't care if I win or lose. I want to meet new people."

Sarah, a Gen-Y player, said, "I never mind losing to a good shot."

That's so cool. Why beat yourself up for a killer shot you can't return? Chances are other people at your level can't return it either!

"You just want to get on the court. So even if you don't know the rules and you're not doing anything right, that's a win," said Stacie Townsend.

Coach M.J. said, "It doesn't matter how well you play. It matters that you play."

Coach Dawson said, "I will walk around a facility, and if someone misses a shot, I make a motion like flushing the toilet. Get rid of it. The happiest pickleball players are those with the shortest memories."

"There are two undeniable truths about competing," he continued, "Someone will always be better than you, and you will always lose again. Those two absolutes will never change."

Affirmations

Another way to keep a positive outlook is to use affirmations. Affirmations are positive self-talk designed to psych you up.

You might remember the character Stuart Smalley from Saturday Night Live. He's the one who said, "I'm good enough. I'm smart enough. And doggone it, people like me."

That's an affirmation.

That character, in real life, was Al Franken. He wound up becoming the U.S. Senator from Minnesota. He won by 312 votes. I wonder where he'd be if he didn't believe in affirmations. They work.

You can psych yourself up for pickleball as well.

Coach Katie told me in a class, "I am a wall. You cannot hit the ball past me. You can hit it hard. You can slam it. You can dink it. You can target me. You can hit it to me all day long. And I will do everything I can to return it. You cannot hit the ball past me."

Wow! That's powerful!

I say that too. It doesn't work as well for me as it does for her. But with practice, I'm sure I will become a wall.

Here's a point to ponder: Stop worrying about what people think about you. Here's the secret: They aren't thinking about you! They are thinking about their games.

"Surfers have a saying, 'All days are good days when you get in the water.' They don't care how big the wave is. I look at pickleball in the same way. As long as you get on the court, all is good," said Coach Dawson. "We are so lucky to play pickleball."

Here are ideas to improve your mental game:

1. Create an affirmation. What can you say to pep yourself up? What's your affirmation?

2. What belief do you have that holds you back? What can you say to turn that negative into a positive?

3. "There is no such thing as a problem. Only a challenge," said Coach Tim.

4. "I never lose. Either I win, or I learn," said Nelson Mandela.

Try these ideas, and you'll have a much better time on the courts!

Everyone Blows a Shot Sometimes

If you miss a shot and lose a point, don't despair. You are not alone.

I've noticed that one thing always happens in a pickleball game...

The rally always ends.

Overcoming Mind Traps

Don't let yourself be bogged down by negative thinking. Use this exercise to overcome your limiting beliefs.

'Mind trap' Example	Mental Reframe
I should have hit that easy shot!!	I know what I did wrong so I won't do that again.
I was lucky to make that shot.	
It's out of my control.	
I can't do it.	
I'm always wrong.	
I'm not going to like it.	
I never get invited to things.	
Pickleball is just too hard for me.	
I'm never going to get better at this.	
I don't want to learn that.	

Pickleball
PUBLISHING COMPANY

Someone blows a shot.

They hit the ball out of bounds.

They swing and miss.

They hit the ball into the net.

The ball bounces twice before they can hit it.

They serve to the wrong court.

There are many more faults, but those are just a few. Everyone makes faults.

New players.

Experienced players.

Even players at pickleball championships.

Everyone misses a shot—eventually.

So, it's no big deal. Just notice what you are doing and seek to improve, so it doesn't happen as often—or ever again. Use the Pickleball Journal in this book to remember what to work on.

Pickleball: The Ultimate Beginner's Guide | 135

Pickleball Journal

Today I focused on:

Date:

How I feel about today:

My act of kindness:

My new friend and phone:

Reason for my rating

Something new I learned today:

Chapter 17
The Body Game: Don't Get Hurt!

Pickleball offers many possible health benefits, ranging from increased agility, stability, hand-eye coordination, flexibility, and maybe even cardio if you run around a lot!

Nate Stier, who owns five physical therapy clinics in suburban Minneapolis, notes the health benefits of pickleball—as well as the risks.

On the positive side, pickleball can help:

Health Improvements - A study in the International Journal of Research in Exercise Physiology found middle-aged and older adults who played one hour of pickleball three days per week for six weeks improved their blood pressure, cholesterol, and cardiorespiratory fitness levels.

Hand-Eye Coordination - As we age, it's normal to see your hand-eye coordination start to decline gradually and it may take time to recognize what is happening. Playing pickleball can help with hand-eye coordination because it requires you to focus on your reaction time and can keep your brain sharp.

Safety Factor - Even though the game can be played outdoors, it is usually played inside, which makes it a great option during those extremely hot summer days. The ball used to play this game is made of plastic, has circular holes, and is hollow, which keeps the travel speed to a moderate level and if the ball happens to hit you, you won't be severely hurt. Also, the net is set to a lower height than in tennis and the serving is always underhanded, which causes less stress on your upper arms and shoulders. The paddle is lighter than a tennis racket, at 7 ounces, which creates low-impact stress on your arms.

But, like any sport, you can get injured if you don't warm up and take care during play.

The Journal of Emergency Medicine estimated 19,000 pickleball injuries in 2017, with 90% affecting people 50 and older.

Nate has seen an uptick in injuries.

"We are seeing more pickleball injuries, that's for sure, as this game becomes more popular," Nate said. "Primarily, we see soft tissue injuries, such as ligament sprains and muscle strains. It can be the lower extremity, quadriceps, hamstrings, Achilles, and calf. I would say most of the conditions that we see are tendinitis based on either the lower extremity or shoulder, wrist, or elbow."

Surprisingly, one problem they don't see is shoulder injuries!

Nate continued, "We don't see as many shoulder injuries in pickleball versus tennis just because it's more of an underhand sport than overhand." There are overhead aspects to pickleball, but not near the frequency or intensity of tennis.

In case you do get injured, Stier also co-founded a medical device company, FiixBody, that invented a medical device to treat tennis and golfer's elbow. This device provides deep tissue massage to the affected area and also comes with a home exercise program to follow. This device and program have been proven successful in clinical trials performed with the assistance of the University of Minnesota.

The patented Kinetic system found in every ProKennex pickleball paddle reduces shock by 43% and vibration by 23%, helping eliminate the epidemic of arm injury and strain in Pickleball. For a list of our recommended products, go to www.pickleballpublishingcompany.com/products

Don't Overdo It

The ease of playing pickleball can also lead to a problem: overuse.

Nate said, "People say, 'I can play pickleball for three hours versus tennis, which I can only play for a half hour because it's a lot more physical. With pickleball, I can play longer. I can play for more days in a row. I play six days a week.' I try to talk to people about knowing their limitations and knowing their bodies. For example, after three hours of pickleball, an athlete's muscles are fatigued, therefore he or she loses some coordination and balance. This can lead to muscle strains, tendonitis, or even tendon ruptures."

Another possible injury is retinal eye detachment.

Coach M.J. said, "I always recommend wearing protective eyewear (indoors and the obvious sunglasses outdoors) and a sturdy brimmed baseball-style hat or visor. I've been hit in the temple and nose numerous times, only centimeters from my eyes, definitely worth wearing solid temple protection eyewear."

Common Pickleball Injuries

Pickleball does have the possibility of injuries and accidents, including general risks such as a fall, bump, or bruise. However, there are common injuries that are more likely to affect pickleball players specifically. Many common pickleball injuries are categorized as overuse injuries, meaning these injuries develop gradually over time due to repeated movements. Here are common injuries noted by Nate.

Shoulder Strain - A common pickleball injury is general shoulder pain, strain, or injury to the rotator cuff. The rotator cuff is an essential structure of the shoulder, supporting the arm at the shoulder joint. While damage to the rotator cuff is possible, one of the most common injuries for pickleball players is a general strain on the shoulder. Overextension of the shoulder can damage the muscles over time and cause pain, inflammation and even reduce your shoulder's full range of motion.

Pickleball Elbow - "Pickleball elbow" is a similar injury to tennis elbow that causes pain when the elbow is overused. Repeated motions like swinging a pickleball paddle can continue to put stress on the elbow over time. If you play pickleball with improper form or training, you're at a higher risk of a potential injury, as poor form can lead to small tears in the elbow's tendons. Pickleball elbow can cause soreness near and around the elbow and aching, stiffness, and pain that worsens with movement.

Heel Bruising - Heel bruising is another common pickleball injury that can develop slowly over time. If the fat pad that surrounds the heel experiences irritation or damage due to repetitive contact and movements, you may develop internal bruising. The heel bone itself may also experience bruising depending on the severity of the injury. Bruising on or inside the heel area and pain that worsens as you apply pressure to the heel is common with this injury.

Achilles Tendonitis - Achilles tendonitis is another overuse injury that can develop from high-impact exercise or repeated stress on the lower leg. In more severe cases, the Achilles tendon may experience multiple tears. There are two forms of Achilles tendonitis, including non-insertional and insertional. Non-insertional Achilles tendonitis affects the middle of the tendon. On the other hand, insertional Achilles tendonitis affects the lower portion of the tendon. Achilles tendonitis symptoms include pain in the calf, swelling of the tendon area and lower leg and heel stiffness.

If you experience an injury while playing pickleball, you'll want to make sure you get proper treatment for the injury.

I'm Okay—I'm Not Okay

When should you see a physical therapist?

Coach Dawson said, "I see my physical therapist every week whether or not I need the attention. I have my exercises and routines I do just to get on the court. I do these routines to try to stay injury free. I do my exercises every day."

While this is excellent preventive care, you might not have the budget or insurance to do that! Here's what a therapist said.

Nate recommends, "If you are sore and fatigued the next day, your body is telling you to take some days of rest. It varies so much by the person. That's why we try to tell them to listen to their own bodies. Don't play through severe fatigue or pain. And if you're sore the next day, try to take some days of rest until your pain subsides before you return to play. If you're sore from playing pickleball, but you can go about your day, and the soreness resolves in less than 48 hours, you're recovering fine. But if the pain lasts more than

24 or 48 hours, or it's affecting your daily activities, see a physical therapist. I would say that once an injury affects your daily life, it's a good time to see a physical therapist."

Not all physical therapists are the same. While very few PTs specialize in pickleball, Stier said you'll want to look for somebody who specializes in sports and orthopedics. He recommends, "Somebody who has a history in treating sports injuries is important."

Preventing Pickleball Injuries

Although the sport a simple, low-stress game, there is a risk of getting injured. Here are some ways to avoid an injury while having some pickleball fun, according to Nate.

Warm-ups for Pickleball

Light Jogging - Start by jogging for five to ten minutes.

Dynamic Stretching - Involves exercises such as lunges, high knees, butt kicks, and leg swings.

Shoulder Rotations - Rotate your shoulders forward and backward, and then lift your arms above your head and circle them in a clockwise and anticlockwise direction.

Arm Swings - Hold your arms out at shoulder height and swing them back and forth, crossing them in front of your chest and then out to the sides.

Squats - Perform a few sets of squats to activate your glutes and other leg muscles. Make sure to keep your back straight and your knees aligned with your toes.

"Remember to start slowly and gradually increase the intensity of your warm-up. By warming up properly, you can help prevent injuries and perform at your best during the game," he said.

Injury Prevention 101: Warm Up!

"I always tell people to think about your ligaments and tendons as pieces of plastic. If they're cold, they're going to be a little bit more brittle. They're going to be less pliable. Once you get them warmed up, they'll stretch a little more. They're going to be damaged less easily. I tell people to warm up to where things are a little bit more flexible," Nate said.

To avoid injuries, he said people should warm up with dynamic exercises which stretch the muscles to their full range of motion. Use the actual movements you would do in a pickleball game.

"Doing something where you get a little bit of sweat going before you exercise is really important. It can be a brisk walk, a light jog, or anything to get the blood flowing," he added.

Coach M.J. said, "I tell everyone to warm up. If you get hurt, you can't play. People say they warm up, but do they really? I always walk them through a few drills to get them warmed up. Warming up is the most important thing I teach all my students to do every single time we play. We don't stretch enough when we play."

Warm-Up Exercises

"Most people sit at a computer for a ton of their day, and it deactivates their glutes. It deactivates muscles we need in pickleball, and in life, and it creates a lot of dysfunction in our bodies," said Coach Clinton.

Here are simple exercises you can do in only a few minutes.

Crab Walk

Pickleball uses sideways motion. "The crab walk prepares you for sideways motion, which is essential in pickleball," said Coach M.J. You'll warm up your glutes and quads.

- Hips square to the net.
- Chin up.
- Goddess pose from Yoga.
- The right foot takes a step.
- The left foot meets it.
- Eyes always look at the opponent.

The Kick Back

"The kickback builds all the small and big muscles you need to be successful and have powerful footwork for pickleball," said Coach Clinton.

Get an elastic band and wrap it around your ankles. The band can't be too tight because you have to stretch it effectively to warm up your muscles.

Kick your leg back in a diagonal motion, ten times on each side.

It's not straight back. It's not straight out to the side.

The Monster Walk

This exercise uses a band also. Pigeon-toe your feet inward. Stand so there's good tension in the band.

Stay really low. Keep your legs bent.

Walk pigeon-toed five to ten steps forward.

Walk five to ten steps backward.

Stay in that position and go sideways, five steps to one side and then five to the other side.

Keep the band nice and tight.

Come back to the center.

If you're not burning enough, you just give a little more tension.

"Those exercises will give you so much more lower body and core strength," said Coach Clinton.

Yoga poses are wonderful for stretching every part of your body (and parts of your body you didn't know you have!) You can find excellent videos at Yoga with Adriene (yogawithadriene.com/free-yoga-videos).

Prevent The Most Common Injury: Don't Backpedal

Running backward or backpedaling can lead to falls. It is one of the most common and devastating injuries in pickleball.

"It is easier to say, 'good shot' than to risk an injury to hit a ball," said Chad Barr, a Baby Boomer pickleball player in suburban Cleveland.

A good coach will discuss safety with new players.

Coach Paranto said, "The very first thing we go over with beginners is safety because we don't want injuries. We don't want them to get hurt and then not be able to play. We won't do lobs, so people won't have to run backward.

"The biggest injury in pickleball of all time is backpedaling, losing your balance, reaching back, and breaking your wrist.

There have even been cases of people backpedaling falling on the wrist, then hitting their head and dying."

Chapter 18
Ready Position/ Athletic Stance

Coach Daniel said he could always spot a newbie, "The new players aren't prepared. They aren't ready. Beginners aren't in 'ready position.' They aren't looking at the server. They aren't watching the ball."

You must be in an athletic stance. "Don't stand like a tree," he said. When you stand straight, you limit your ability to run and move.

When playing pickleball, standing in a position that allows you to reach the ball and hit it effectively is important. Here are some general guidelines to get into ready stance (a.k.a. "athletic stance"), so you can move quickly and generate power when hitting the ball:

- Stand with your feet shoulder-width apart, with your weight evenly distributed over both feet.

- Bend your knees slightly, so you are flexible. How far you can bend depends on your body mechanics, but some bend is better than none.

- Move your feet apart. How far is up to you. Be comfortable.

- Put your weight lightly forward toward your toes if you can. You cannot run if your weight is on your heels.

- Keep your body facing the direction of the ball, with your arms extended in front of you. This will help you reach for the ball and hit it.

- Be ready to move to the ball at all times. Keep your eyes on the ball and be prepared to step in any direction to reach it.

READY POSITION

NOT-READY POSITION

NO, YOU'RE NOT BOTHERING ME. WHAT'S UP?

- If you are at the kitchen line, hold the paddle at the 11 o'clock position (or 1 o'clock for lefties) at face height if you are at the net because the ball will be high.

- If you are at the baseline or in no-man's-land, hold the paddle's heel directly in front of your belly button because the ball will come in low. If the paddle is in the middle, you can quickly move the paddle to hit your forehand or backhand. "If the paddle is by your side, you will lose precious seconds to hit the ball properly. It takes too long to come up and hit the ball," said Coach Jimbo. Coach Tim said, "It's not a matter of seconds. It's a matter of milliseconds."

The most important point is to be comfortable and balanced, so you will be able to move quickly and hit the ball effectively.

Now, you can move around the court and hit the ball effectively.

Tom Corson-Knowles, a Gen-X pickleball player in Indiana, said, "Understanding body mechanics and the kinetic chain is really important. You need to know how to move your body most efficiently to maintain stability and generate power and consistency in your shots. Understanding body mechanics and ensuring your feet, hips, and entire body are aligned will help you increase your stability when taking shots, which will make you a better player while reducing your risk of injury too!"

Look at your stance:

- Do you have a solid base?
- Are your feet spread apart?
- Are your knees bent?

Chapter 19
Footwork

Proper footwork will save you from a fall and help you get to the ball faster.

Coach Clinton stated, "Footwork is the number one thing to work on as a new player. Not hand speed. It's footwork. That's because 85% of the equation is solved when you get your footwork right. You find yourself in the right position on the court at the right time, and your shots become easier."

If you can run to the ball, you have time to set up to take an excellent shot. If you aren't in the proper position, you'll probably lunge at the ball and use your arm, which can create a bad angle and lead to a fault.

Here's how to improve your game by improving your footwork.

Coach Katie said, "Footwork is being in position at the right place at the right time. You're in the ready stance, which is a wider stance, on your toes so your weight is going forward, and not in your heels so you can move more easily. Your paddle is up in front of you. I like to say at eleven o'clock if you're right-handed or at one o'clock if you're a lefty. Favor your backhand a little bit. Every time you do a shot, you're coming back to your ready position. So, you're back in a wide stance on your toes and reset your paddle every time. Reset and reset and reset."

Be aware of your lateral movement.

"In pickleball, we should move forward and kind of side to side. I call it a crab shuffle across the court. That's how I teach lateral movement, side to side across the court. Then our momentum is going forward. We are transitioning momentum from our back foot to our front foot with all of our shots. It's a matter of shuffling and cutting off edges. I try to help people avoid falling by using the lateral movement to dance around the court."

Don't cross one foot over the other. That's not as efficient or safe as the crab walk.

Coach Paranto said, "Footwork is important. You need to prepare early. As soon as your opponent hits the ball, you should start moving to the area of the court where the ball is going so that when you hit the ball, you can be still. I don't want people running through shots."

Watch This!
www.PickleballPublishingCompany.com/Footwork

Chapter 20
Fully Armed

Let's not forget your arms.

Coach Paranto said, "The wrist should never move. When the wrist flicks, the angle of the paddle changes from open to close or close to open. It's really hard to control the ball."

One arm position can help you perform many shots.

Coach Clinton said, "When we have a solid base and use our shoulder, we can use the laws of physics to backswing and follow through. We don't have to swing hard if we want to hit harder. We need to backswing more and follow through more. In pickleball, we want to have the least number of moving parts in our body. Only flex your shoulder. Use your shoulder to lift the ball over.

"If you think about a tank, a tank has a turret. And when you raise the turret, the cannonball goes higher and shorter distances. And if you lower your turret, the ball goes lower on a line drive and goes longer distances. So if you think about holding the ball like a turret and you pop the ball up, you are raising the turret, and you hit the ball too high. If you lower the turret, you can hit a nice line drive. If I want to hit a higher ball, I raise the turret a little bit and do the same motion."

This analogy works for many types of shots.

"I teach a real simple serve: the underhand serve," he continued. "It's kind of like the game of Cornhole (a game like ring toss or horseshoes wherein you toss a bean bag into a hole). It's a simple underhand toss. You might try tossing a ball like a cornhole bag to get the muscle memory locked into your body for a serve, for a third shot drive to the kitchen, and for dinking. It's all the same motion."

There's a strategic benefit to this motion.

"The other team does not know what the serve will look like because I'm making the same motion. For a third-shot drop, I move up a little bit closer and use the same motion and less backswing. When I dink, I use the same motion but go up a little closer. You have the same muscle memory, so you're going to have exponential gains in your game instead of trying to do a different shot from every part of the court. You can disguise which shot you're doing because it's the same motion. This doesn't mean you'll never have a different style of shot. But the more shots you can have that are the same motion, and it will be more predictable. Quiet the joints in your arm, so you use only one joint to lift the ball over the net. We eliminate much of the margin for error because only one joint moves," Coach Clinton said.

Chapter 21
The Eyes Have It

Has this happened to you? You see a ball coming towards you. It is nice and slow and bounces nicely. You can't wait to smack the ball! You swing—and your paddle misses entirely! What happened?

You took your eyes off the ball.

"Beginners look for where the ball is going to go right before impact. They look where they want to hit the ball," said Coach Paranto. "We don't want that happening. The court never moves. You're going to use your peripheral vision and awareness to locate where you want the ball to go. I want your eyes to be watching that ball hit your paddle's sweet spot. The closer your head is to your paddle head and impact, the more likely you are to hit that sweet spot."

Coach Katie agrees. "Get in ready position. Watch the ball. I'm trying to create tunnel vision so that I just watch the ball. Some people will say watch for the holes in the ball so that I'm not distracted by other things in the court."

Visualize This!

"If you play golf, you keep your eye on the ball as it sits on the tee or on the ground. You swing and see the club hit the ball. Then you move your head to see where the ball is going. You should look at the ball just like a golfer does," said Coach Jimbo. "You should see the pickleball hit your paddle. Then look to see where the ball goes."

Chapter 22
Shake Hands with Your New Best Friend: Your Paddle

How do you hold a paddle?

Simply shake hands with it.

As you progress, you'll use slightly different grips, but for now, shake hands.

"We start with beginners just finding a grip they can hit both forehand and backhand with without switching grips," said Coach Paranto. "It is between a continental grip and a forehand grip, a shake-hands grip. That's the main thing. I'll catch people switching to a backhand grip and then a forehand grip, and they can't keep up when the rally changes."

Coach Paranto continued, "I teach grip pressure because grip pressure is huge. If you have a scale of one to ten with ten being tight and one being relaxed, then in between every shot, I want the grip to be a one because your hands move way quicker. When you dink, we're pretty soft. We're about a two. We're just lifting. We're not doing any aggressive dinks yet. We're just arching dinks."

Take a small backswing and a small follow-through. That way, you'll be ready for the return after you hit the ball.

Coach M.J. advises, "You need a tighter grip when you serve, closer to a ten."

Watch This! *Three tips to improve your dinking with Coach Tim and Spencer Laurent on PickleballTV: www.PickleballPublishingCompany.com/dink*

PART 3
Get Strategic

When I first started playing pickleball, I was happy just to hit the ball over the net. But after I lost 100 or so games, I realized there was more to the game.

As you continue your journey, you'll realize the better players know something you don't: strategy.

You've read strategies for serving and returning the ball throughout this book. You'll discover a few more interesting strategies in this section to help you become a better player. There's more to learn, but these tactics will help you at the beginning stages.

"Pickleball is a game of adding skills," according to David Lee, who describes himself as "just an intermediate player who pays attention at clinics and observes players who are better than me to see what makes them successful."

Here are the basics:

- Get your serve in consistently.
- Return deep consistently.
- Move to the net quickly and consistently.
- Keep your paddle up in front of you.
- Add on to your game as you get good at the basics.

"The one thing I wish I knew when I started was that 80-year-old ladies can and will kick my a$$ all over the court," said Lee. "I believe it is important to play a lot of open pickleball to get all kinds of touches and advice from other players."

The two lessons I learned from David are to never judge a player by his or her appearance and play as many games as possible. There is no substitute for playing games.

Important Strategic Tips

1. The serving team will want to stand behind the baseline because your opponents want to hit the ball deep to keep you back. Your paddle should be waist-high and centered because the returning shot probably will be waist-high or lower, so you'll have more time to react to the ball and hit a good shot. The serving team should stay near the baseline to return the second shot, as opponents will want to keep you back. "Your goal is to get to the kitchen as fast as feasible," said Coach M.J. If you run too

soon, your opponents are in a good position to hit the ball by you as you run up! Coach Charlie said you must "earn the right" to get to the kitchen. How do you do that? When your opponents hit the ball short, you can claim that territory and move closer to the kitchen.

2. As the defending player, you will want to return a serve softly in an arc or softly, so you can run to the kitchen. You have less time to get to the net if you hit the ball hard. "If you're short or have a hip or knee that's been replaced (which happens to many players), you want to give yourself time to get up there," said Coach Jimbo.

3. The returner at the kitchen should stand close to the kitchen line. "Most people don't even start in the right position at the kitchen. People want to start two feet back from the kitchen line. No matter how much I tell them, they start in the wrong position," said Coach Tim. "But it takes a lifetime for some of these people to get there. And so that's important." An adage is, "The team that controls the net controls the game." Many new players are afraid of the kitchen. Remember, something good is cooking in the kitchen.

4. When you are at the kitchen, hold your paddle at the eleven o'clock position (slightly to the left of your head) if you're a righty or one o'clock position if you're a lefty. Your arm should extend forward slightly so you can hit balls more quickly and have a longer reach. You will have more time to return a ball hit hard at you. "If your

arm is close to your body, it's a disaster. Your arm must be forward, but not so far forward that you can't do anything with it. There's a bend, and it's definitely forward," said Coach Tim. "Adopt a low, athletic stance. Position the rim of the paddle in line with your eyes so you can track the ball properly—and remind you to reset to ready position after each shot."

5. Moving in tandem with your partner is an essential part of the game. "If you can't see your partner, you're in trouble!" said Coach Charlie. When you are serving, both players stand behind the baseline. As you have the opportunity to move up, do so in line with your partner. If she moves up, so should you. If you are both at the net and one partner runs to the sideline to return a dink, the other partner should shuffle in that direction to cover the area the partner left open. Chances are, the returning shot will be in the closer court, so you need to guard that area. If you don't cover that area, your opponent could get an easy point.

6. Practice your serve. A good serve can set you up for success in a pickleball game, so it's important to work on your technique. Practice serving from different positions on the court and try to get a feel for how much spin you need to put on the ball to get it to go where you want it to.

7. Focus on placement. In pickleball, placement is often more important than power. Try to hit the ball to areas of

the court where your opponents are not positioned and try to anticipate where they will hit the ball next.

8. Keep your eye on the ball. Staying focused and keeping your eye on the ball at all times is important, as the ball can move quickly in pickleball. Try to move your feet to get into position to hit the ball and be ready to adjust your shot as needed.

9. Learn the rules. Familiarize yourself with the rules of pickleball, as this will help you understand the game better and make it easier to play.

10. Have fun. Pickleball is a great sport for all ages, and it's important to remember that the most important thing is to have fun. Don't get too caught up in winning or losing, and just enjoy the game.

Chapter 23
The 75% Paradox: Pickleball's Dirty Little Secret

I was shocked to read an article that said 75% of all rallies end with unforced errors! That's a shot the opponent misses because of his or her own mistake and not because of the opponent's skill.

Maybe she took her eyes off the ball. Perhaps she wanted to slam the ball, but it went into the net instead. Perhaps she tried to finesse a serve, and it backfired. Or she hit the ball too hard, and it landed out. Perhaps she thought her partner would hit the ball but didn't because he thought she would.

"If you just get the ball over the net one more time than they do, you win," said Coach Clinton. "Let them make a mistake. Induce mistakes by getting the ball over the net one more time than they do, preferably in an unattackable spot."

Coach Barrett said, "Realize that pickleball is a game of error avoidance. Pickleball is all about surviving on the court until your opponent makes a mistake. Forcing your opponents to make mistakes is the primary way of winning."

Good defenses will win games.

A common problem with many players—even advanced players—is they have no patience. They want to slam everything. However, the ball often goes into the net or flies out of bounds. You have more time to hit the ball than you might think. "Be patient!" said Coach Tim.

The bottom line is you don't have to be fancy or powerful to win in pickleball. You just have to avoid unforced errors. Just hit the ball over the net. Let the other team make mistakes.

Forcing Errors

How can you force your opponent to make mistakes? Here are simple strategies any beginner can use to win points.

- If the ball is high, let it fly. Most balls that come at your head will probably land out of bounds. Let the ball fly out, so you win the point.

- Down the middle solves the riddle. When you hit the ball down the middle of the court, your opponents might think the other person will get the ball. Sometimes, neither player will hit the ball—especially if the team has bad communication. This shot is called, humorously, the "divorce shot." Let your partner know if you can get it—or if he should. Communication is key. "Beginners go for the lines too much. They can turn a winner into a loser, that can turn a match around," said Coach Paranto.

- "Isolate the weaker player," said Coach Paranto.

- "Aim for their feet. It is hard to return that shot," said Coach M.J.

- Hit the ball to your opponent's backhand, which is usually his or her weaker side.

- Hit the ball so the other team has to run. It is hard to hit and run. "If I can get them moving, you disrupt the base. And contrary to some thinking, we get our accuracy and control not from our arms or hands, but from our base; from our legs and foot positioning," said Coach Clinton. "Get your opponents moving. Place the ball over to the right. Then place it to the left. Make them move back and forth. If I keep going back and forth, eventually, they're either going to hit a bad shot because they're moving or they're going to forget to go back to the middle, so you'll have an opening to hit the ball down the middle."

This strategy reminds me of the best quote in baseball strategy (which applies to pickleball), "Hit the ball where they ain't."

If you can keep your opponents moving, you can keep your score grooving.

Red Light, Green Light: Reduce Your Errors

"You can prevent your errors using the 'Stoplight System' to select your shot," said Coach M.J.

Red is a shot at your feet: reset. Just get the ball back over the net. Sometimes this means just getting your paddle down at the correct angle and returning to position.

Yellow is net height. This is better than body parts as players' heights vary. Take a shot to set up your next shot. Be patient.

Green is enough above the net for a definite "put-away" (vs. a shot above your waist.) Go for the winner.

Bottom line is this: put the ball in play, and good things can happen.

Watch This!

www.PickleballPublishingCompany.com/ShouldILetTheBallBounce

Chapter 24
The Kitchen Is Cooking!

You've heard the phrase, "If you can't stand the heat, get out of the kitchen."

The opposite is true in pickleball.

"Controlling the kitchen is how you win," said Coach Paranto.

But getting newbies to believe this is another thing.

Many newer players are afraid to stand next to the kitchen line. They might be concerned about getting hit by the ball! Or they aren't confident in their dinking game. Or they just like to play deep, as they might have done if they played tennis. You need to get over this fear. As you play more, drill more, practice more, and take more lessons, you will come to enjoy your time at the net. Plus, you won't have to run around as much.

"A lot of players are afraid of getting drilled at the net," said Coach Tim.

Coach Pam said, "I yell at people to get to the net. Go. Go. Go. I pair them with an experienced player, so I know they will hit the ball back to them. Then they slam the ball and win a point. People say, 'That was just fabulous. I want to do that again.' I say, 'Now do you see why I told you to go to the net?'"

Stacie Townsend, founder of *The Pickler*, said, "I think people stay back because of the speed. The kitchen line can be intimidating. When I started, I was like, 'Oh, I'm going to stay back at the baseline.' I stayed back because I thought it'd be easier to run around and keep the ball over the net. I didn't understand the nuance of the kitchen. They feel like they have more time, and I think there's an intimidation factor playing at the net."

Remember, the team that controls the kitchen controls the game.

Chapter 25
Beat the Bangers!

Bangers are people who slam the ball back and forth.

"Bangers are ruining the game of pickleball for the newbie," said Coach Clinton jokingly. "Bangers usually win because they have something that some of us that don't play tennis don't have: hard, fast groundstrokes. It's difficult to defend, and it's frustrating as hell."

Coach Clinton continued, "This can sometimes set a poor example for new players because we learn by watching. We learn by example. Newbies are unconsciously learning they need to hit hard to win. That is not the only pathway. The pathway to success is to learn how to hit the ball in a way that is un-attackable. That means placement over power."

You can beat bangers with dinks.

Have a soft, solid base.

Use your shoulder.

Lift the ball over.

Hit the ball in a place that is unattackable.

"Have patience. Don't attack every ball," he said. "Make that banger have to hit a dink because they're going to hit the ball into the net. Bangers hate dink rallies because they don't know how to dink, okay? They know how to bang. So become a great dinker. But first, you need to become a great third-shot dropper because that induces the dink rally."

If you are in open play and will be paired with a banger or against a banger, it is okay to move your paddle, so you don't play with him or her.

Watch This!
www.PickleballPublishingCompany.com/BeatTheBangers

Beat the Banger Drill

Here's an easy drill to help you beat bangers.

"Lift the pizza," Coach M.J. said, referring to the pickleball and the paddle as the pizza spatula. "This is not a swing. Get your paddle under the ball, so the ball goes into the kitchen. You will beat the banger. That will frustrate the bangers. It works magically."

Chapter 26
Pickleball, Anyone? Tips for Tennis Players

Many tennis players now play pickleball. While some similarities exist between the two sports, tennis players need to know certain things to win at pickleball.

"Tennis players need to break bad habits and learn new skills," said Coach M.J.

The good news is there's less running in pickleball. If you had to give up tennis because you are running out of steam or your knees are giving out, you'll enjoy pickleball, especially doubles.

The serve is crucial in tennis, but not so much in pickleball.

Don't try to ace your serve. Pickleball rules take away the advantage of the server. The ball must bounce before the receiver can hit the ball. Save your power shots for later. However, you can add topspin, backspin, and side spin to your serves to confuse your opponents.

"If you're a tennis player, we will not change that much. We're going to keep much of your groundstroke," said Coach M.J. "Dinking is foreign to a tennis player."

The biggest change tennis players must adjust to is the backswing. Tennis requires a big backswing. Pickleball does not.

"You don't need a big backswing," said Coach M.J. "A long backswing will hurt your game as you'll lose valuable time to hit the ball. To correct this, stand in front of a wall with your back to the wall. Take your normal swing. Now move closer to the wall so your arm can't go that far back. Your muscle memory will realize where your swing should be."

Oh yes, one more thing.

You don't need to wear a fancy tennis dress. Pickleball players are pretty informal. Of course, if you want to wear your tennis outfit, you can.

PART 4
Get Better

You can learn a lot by reading books, watching videos, and viewing video courses. But if you want to get better, you need to work with a coach. Only an experienced coach can see what you are doing wrong. These coaches can suggest you make subtle adjustments that can mean the difference between winning points or sending the ball out of bounds. In this section, you'll discover different ways to work with a pickleball professional so you can improve your game.

"I was going to suggest we all go for chicken wings, but I don't want to insult Bob."

Chapter 27
What Level Are You?

Everyone wants to know how he or she compares to others.

There is the subjective way of comparison and the objective way of comparison.

The subjective way says, "I make a good shot!" "I blew that one." "I gotta improve my backhand." This way is fraught with peril as you introduce self-doubt and criticism on the one hand and an overabundance of confidence and euphoria on the other.

The objective way takes the emotion out of the equation. You either get better at a skill, or you hold firm. This method helps you get better without beating yourself up.

Let's look at an objective way to determine your skill level and your progress. Pickleball has an official rating system that ranges from 1.0 (beginner with no knowledge of pickleball) to 5.0 expert. These ratings come in handy when you want to play in a league or find players of similar abilities.

You'll start as a 1.0 player, a newbie. After a short time, as you learn the rules and the play of the game, you'll be a 2.0 or 2.5. Notice that the scale moves by half a point. Intermediates are 3.0. As you increase your knowledge and skill, you will move up the ladder of progress.

For example, ask yourself:

1. Do I know the rules?

2. Can I serve consistently?

3. Can I dink accurately?

4. Do my forehand and backhand shots land inside the court consistently?

5. Can I return a fast volley?

6. Can I return a shot that has a spin?

7. Do I know the essential strategies?

You can find the official rating sheet with the skills at the U.S.A. Pickleball site:

www.usapickleball.org/tournaments/tournament-player-ratings/player-skill-rating-definitions/

You can also see how you compare by joining a ladder league at a club. You'll play games against each other and keep score. After a few games, you'll have a good idea of your level.

Chapter 28
Diary of a Successful Pickleball Player

Your Personal Journal

I created this assessment to help you improve game by game. You can list the date, the weather (sunny, cloudy, windy, etc.), and the location. You can list what you did well and what you need to work on. Notice, I didn't write the negative (what didn't work) or anything else that introduces negative self-talk. Focus on your best moment, like a terrific serve or a masterful dink.

You can use the sheet on page 182 to keep track of your progress. You can copy this sheet or download copies at: www.PickleballPublishingCompany.com/formsto.

Pickleball Journal

Today I focused on:

Date:

How I feel about today:

My act of kindness:

Reason for my rating

My new friend and phone:

Something new I learned today:

Your Rating Scorecard

The "wheel of life" is a standard measuring tool used by life coaches. On page 184, I built on this structure to create a tool you can use to measure your improvement. You'll see a circle divided into eight segments. Each segment represents a skill you can measure and would like to improve, like serving, dinking, and backhand.

For each skill, you'll see ten segments, numbered one to ten. Rate yourself for each skill. If you mastered the skill, give yourself a ten. If you are new, you might give yourself a one or a two.

After 30 days, rate yourself again. Take a different colored pen or pencil to fill in your new level.

After 60 days, rate yourself again.

After 90 days, rate yourself again.

You'll see a colorful chart that shows your progress.

Where are you today? Fill in the grid and see where you are—and what you need to work on.

How have you progressed in 30 days? Fill in the circle so you can see your progress!

How have you improved in 90 days? Fill in the circle so you can see your progress.

Pickleball — MY PICKLEBALL RATINGS SCORECARD

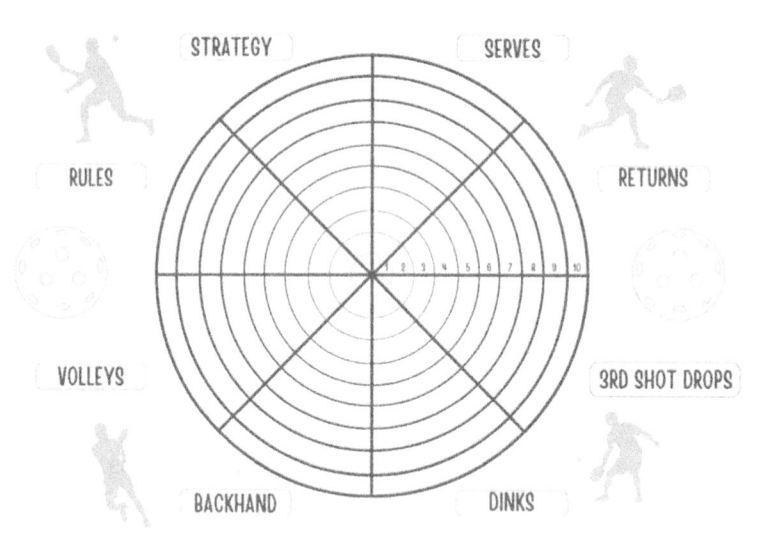

- STRATEGY
- SERVES
- RETURNS
- 3RD SHOT DROPS
- DINKS
- BACKHAND
- VOLLEYS
- RULES

GAME BY GAME

DATE:

Use this form to see what you need to work on and see how far you've come!

Date: _____ Weather: _____ Location: _____

	What I did well	What I need to work on	Partner/ opponents
Game 1			
Game 2			
Game 3			
Game 4			
Game 5			
Game 6			
Game 7			
Game 8			
Game 9			

Pickleball

Chapter 29
What to Expect When You Attend a Lesson or a Clinic

Intro lessons and clinics are terrific ways to start your pickleball journey on the right foot. Clubs and community centers offer classes for a minimal fee. Check online calendars for schedules.

The Intro Lesson

If you are new to pickleball, take an intro lesson with a coach so you can start your pickleball journey on the right foot. The class might be free or very low cost.

In your first lesson, you'll learn the athletic stance, how to hold the paddle, where to stand for different plays, how to keep score, the rules, and other basics. You will play a game with other class members, so you get a feel for all the material you learned. You won't remember all of it! That's why you are reading this book.

Clinics

Clinics focus on core skills, like serving, dinking, driving, and strategy. However, some coaches wing it. They see what level the class is and create drills that will help thos students. Don't expect a great deal of individual attention. There are too many people and not enough time. After all, this is not an individual lesson. However, you will learn from others. You'll see you are not the only person making a mistake. That can be helpful as well. You will leave the lesson with better skills and you will meet nice people.

Chapter 30
Going from Good to Great on the Pickleball Court: Get a Coach

You can learn to play the guitar from a book. However, you need a teacher to listen to ensure you keep the right tempo and hit the right chords. You need a teacher to use their intuition and knowledge to see what you don't see so you can reach the next level.

The same is true with pickleball.

While this pickleball book can teach you the fundamentals and serve as a ready reference guide, only a knowledgeable, caring coach can turn the information you are reading—and the videos you might watch—into actionable skills.

"If you don't get a coach, you will get really good at playing badly," said Coach Tim.

That's because you will reinforce bad habits and will never learn the proper way to play the game.

Coaches might suggest a subtle change in your body mechanics that can profoundly affect your game. When I took a lesson with Coach Charlie, I was missing dinks below my waist. He told me to tilt or turn my wrist in a certain way. Suddenly, a new, wide range of motion was open to me. I dinked the ball back every time. A small movement like this made a significant impact on my game. I never would have figured this out on my own.

You might think you are doing something correctly, but your coach might see that you are not.

Coach M.J. explained that "YouTube can't correct what you're doing wrong, which you'll continue to do wrong—reinforcing the bad habit or poor muscle memory until a coach (or someone you'll listen to who knows the correct form) corrects or teaches you the proper form or technique."

How to Find a Coach

You can find a coach at your pickleball club, community center, or on a local Facebook pickleball forum. Ask your pickleball buddies if they can recommend a coach.

Coach M.J. said, "You learn from different teachers. The best teachers are the ones who give good directions their players can relate to and implement."

Coach Jimbo added, "When getting a coach, you must feel comfortable with them. Chemistry is everything in a relationship, whether it be romance or coaching."

How Can You Get the Most Out of a Lesson?

"Come ready to play and have lots of fun," said Coach Charlie. "Bring a notepad to write tips."

Go to the session with a clear goal, so you don't waste your time and money. What do you want to learn?

If you don't have a goal, don't worry. A good coach will know what to do.

Coach Tim said, "In less than a minute, if I watch you play, I'll know things you should do, and I'll know what to do next. Are you practicing good or bad habits? Most people practice bad habits, and they will never get better. They get really good at being bad. They don't take time to really understand or to study the game."

Sign up for several individual or small group classes to learn skills to improve your game. No matter how good you are or how good you become, there is always another skill you can improve.

And, of course, play as many games as you can. There is no substitute for playing games.

Drinking from a Firehose: How to Remember Your Lesson

The hardest part of any lesson is how to remember all those things you learned!

Write your big takeaways on a notepad or use the voice recorder on your phone to speak your notes. You could also ask your instructor to repeat the key points and demonstrate them as you video them.

I created the "Coaching Diary" on page 193 to track your progress with your coach. Write the date, the coach's name, and the three skills you want to work on. Add notes, so you don't forget the important tips your coach teaches you and the insights you learned.

You might also want to write notes about the coach. Did you like working with him or her? What didn't you like (if anything)? For example, was he patient? Were the instructions clear? Was he focused on helping you, or was he checking his email? Did you feel a connection?

"For today's coaching session, I brought along my stenographer."

Pickleball Coaching Diary

SKILL 1

TIPS	INSIGHTS

SKILL 2

TIPS	INSIGHTS

SKILL 3

TIPS	INSIGHTS

Chapter 31
Perfect Practice Makes Perfect: Get a Drill Partner

Coach Clinton asked ten pro players, "How do you get to the next level? They said something that absolutely blew my mind. They said, 'You have to practice and drill 60% to 70% of the time and only play games 30% to 40% of the time.' If you think about professional football players, what do they do all week? They watch the game tape and practice all week to play a two-hour game. You actually have to practice more than you play. Now, most people aren't willing to do that because they just have fun playing. But if you did that, you get injured a lot less, and you'd get way better, way faster."

Why would it be any different in pickleball?

In pickleball, you must drill if you want to improve.

Teachers and coaches are terrific, but they can get expensive! If you find a drill partner to practice with, you can save money, improve your game, and have fun. You might find a good drill partner from your group lesson with a coach. Or post a notice on Facebook.

Coach Paranto suggested, "Find a drill partner who wants to improve as much as you do. I can't stress more or enough how important it is to have a drill partner that's willing to improve just like you are and just to work on whatever skill you're going to work on."

You can also practice against a wall. Coach Jimbo said, "It is best to have a second person because it is more fun." In either case, take a lot of balls so you can spend more time practicing and less time herding balls.

There's so much to work on. How can you organize your drills?

"Pick one thing to work on every time you go out to play and focus on that," said Coach M.J.

Mary Kelly, Ph.D., an expert in organizational leadership and a new pickleball player in Denver said, "Trying to make massive changes all at once usually leads to burnout or failure. But taking small baby steps with tiny habits toward a bigger goal is doable, sustainable, and puts us on the road to success. Little tweaks can change your life. Take a moment and think about what you could accomplish in a week, a month, or even a year. What could you accomplish if you created tiny habits today and kept building them up over time?"

Drills can be more fun than games. There's something cool about working with your partner and hitting 20 dinks in a row. Here are my favorite drills.

Serving Drills

These easy drills will help you create serves that consistently hit the mark.

Serving Drill 1

Find an open court to practice. Hit six balls into one court. Then retrieve the balls and serve the balls back. Keep track of how many go in and how many go out. I'll bet you will hit the ball into the correct court 100% of the time within a few minutes! If you blow a serve now and then, join the club. Everyone blows a serve.

As your skills progress, aim for different parts of the court so that you can keep your opponents on their toes. Vary your serves: hit short, long, hard, and soft. Aim for your opponent's backhand, which is usually weaker. Serve the ball short, so your opponent needs to run to return the ball. Many people have trouble hitting a ball when they run.

At a beginner level, you'll have a lot of tools to keep your opponents guessing. As you progress, you'll add spins, slices, and power.

Serving Drill 2

Put three cones two feet from the baseline in the right service court. Stand behind the baseline of your right service court. Aim for each cone. You will improve the depth and the targeting of your serves.

Serving Drill 3

You serve the ball to your partner so you can see how your serve looks with an opponent on the other side of the net. Your partner hits the ball back to you easily. You grab the ball and serve again. This drill will help you develop your serve. Your partner will practice hitting the ball deep. And you won't waste time rounding up balls.

Serve from each side of the court so you can get a feel for distinct movements, stances, and perspectives.

After a few minutes, let your partner serve, so she gets practice serving, and you get practice returning.

How to Hit a Dink: The Pancake Dinking Drill

Stand at the kitchen in a ready stance.

Pretend the ball is a pancake and your paddle is the spatula. With the ball in front of you, keep the paddle face open and gently lift the pancake (ball) with your shoulder, arm, and wrist, acting as one unit. Do not use a backswing. Lift with your knees.

"Use a light grip," said Coach M.J. "Say a three out of ten. If you use a tight grip, the ball will pop high, and your opponents will slam the ball back at you for an easy win."

If pancakes aren't your thing, imagine the ball is an egg. You don't want to break the egg!

Coach Paranto said, "When we're dinking, we're not transferring weight."

When you drill with a partner, try hitting ten balls back and forth. Then 20. Then 40. This drill will help your dinking game. As you advance, aim the ball a foot or so to your partner's side so she must move. She dinks the ball to you, and you must move a few feet. Do this the length of the net and then go back and forth along the net. This drill will help your aim and your footwork.

You can also practice dinking the ball cross-court into the kitchen. This is a powerful shot that can gain points.

The Hand-Eye Coordination Drill

Most errors occur when you take your eye off the ball or misjudge where the ball will hit your paddle. With this drill, you can improve your hand-eye coordination.

Hold your paddle in front of you, with the paddle face pointing up. Bounce the ball once. Then twice. Then five times. This is NOT as easy as it looks!

Hit ten times.

Now 20 times.

Then 30 times.

Don't be dismayed if this takes some time!

When you are comfortable doing this, try hitting the ball once and then turning your wrist and paddle over and hitting the ball. Then flip your hand and paddle back and forth as you hit the ball.

Your accuracy will improve when you play a game.

Punch Drill

Stand opposite your drill partner at the kitchen line in ready position. Keep the ball in the air by punching the ball with your paddle at your partner, who will punch the ball back to you. Try for ten volleys. Keeping the ball in the air is difficult, so don't be disappointed if this drill seems hard.

WHAT I NEED TO WORK ON

I am going to work on:

Why I chose this activity:

How do I feel today?

Who am I playing with?

Drills

Notes

Pickleball
PUBLISHING COMPANY

Chapter 32
Lights! Camera! Action: How to Get the Most from a Video

There are so many videos about pickleball on YouTube it is easy to get overwhelmed with information. How can you get the most out of the videos? How can you find the best videos?

Coach Barrett said, "When you're researching things on the internet, you must understand that everything has to be presented to you because they're trying to cast the widest net possible. So, you have to understand that not everything in the video will apply to you. And that's okay. You're not watching the video to learn everything in the video. You're watching the video to figure out what applies to you. I would try to focus on one thing to work on after you watch the video. And then go out and try to get good at that one thing. The last thing you want to do is just fill your head up with a whole bunch of things you've got to do. If you try a whole bunch of stuff, you're not going to get good at all of them all at once. So, focus on one thing."

Chapter 33
Easy Solutions to Common Problems

Problem: The ball doesn't go where I want it to go.

Solution: "Keep your eye on the ball until the paddle hits it," said Coach Tim. "I like to use the acronym WAM: WATCH the hit. ASSESS the shot. MOVE accordingly. I'm talking about *every hit*. Yours. Your partner's. And the other teams' shots."

Coach M.J. said, "It is best if you can anticipate where the ball is going to go. Keep your eyes open and prepare to move to where you think the ball will go."

Coach Clinton said, "Remember that most of your inaccuracy in pickleball is due to either being in the wrong position on the court or not having your feet and body in the right position, therefore creating an unstable base from which you're striking the ball."

Coach Paranto said, "Point the paddle face and wrist to the spot you want to hit."

"Wherever the paddle face is facing is where the ball will go," said Coach Charlie.

Problem: I pop up the ball at the net, and my opponent slams the ball back.

Mistake: "You are gripping the paddle too hard," said Coach M.J.

Solution: "If you use a one to ten scale, with ten being a tight grip, you might use a seven to ten pressure. Use a level two or three pressure instead. You might have been gripping the paddle too tightly. Loosen your grip," she said.

Watch This! *www.PickleballPublishingCompany.com/PopUps*

Problem: I am late getting to balls.

Mistake: You are out of position.

Solution: Get in position.

When you see what your opponent is trying to do, you can get ready to be in a position to return the ball. Your eyes should be on the ball from the moment it leaves your opponent's paddle to the time you hit the ball with your paddle.

"People miss balls because they use their arms instead of their legs," said Coach Tim. "Most people will just reach with their arms. They'll just be out of position. Why not use your footwork to get in a better position? If you're in the correct position, you can place the ball well. That's the next step."

Remember the WAM formula in the tip about hitting the ball where you want it to go.

He continued, "Be prepared to move once you realize where the ball will go. Don't wait until it gets there to move. This sounds obvious, but beginning players wait too long. Even two seconds can be too long. You'll miss the shot. Get your paddle in position and run!"

Problem: My opponents target my weak backhand.

Mistake: If your opponents see you have a weak backhand (as many players have), they'll hit the ball to your backhand all day long.

Solution: "You have to position yourself so you can take more of those balls with your forehand," said Coach Tim. "Or, more importantly, practice better footwork to receive the ball in a more favorable hitting position."

Most players' backhand will be their weakest side. Some players run around the ball so they can use their forehand. This will waste time. "This will immediately be a 'tell' to the opposing team to hit to your backhand."

Better yet, practice your backhand with your drill partner or with a wall, so you'll become a much better player.

Coach CJ Johnson says you can develop your backhand by starting with dinking with your backhand. "Use your shoulder," she said, "not your wrist or your elbow." As you get comfortable with this stroke, move further and further away from the kitchen, and keep practicing.

Watch This!
www.PickleballPublishingCompany.com/Backhand

Problem: I hit the ball out of bounds.

Mistake: Your paddle face is pointing out of bounds.

Solution: Pay attention to your paddle face.

Mistake: You are hitting the ball too late.

Solution: You need to hit the ball when it is a bit in front of you.

"In pickleball, everything should be hit out front," said Coach Paranto. "In tennis, balls are sometimes hit more on the side of you."

Mistake: Your wrist isn't firm.

Solution: Keep a solid wrist to prevent balls from going wide.

Coach Paranto continued, "The reason balls are going in and out all over the crazy place is mainly because people are using their wrists. So, at the moment of impact with the paddle, they only have a slight area of success because their wrist is moving. The wrist should never move. When the wrist flicks, the angles of the paddle change from open to close or close to open. It's really hard to control the ball."

Visualize This!

Imagine someone tosses you a ball, and you catch it. That's where your paddle should connect with the ball.

Put down your paddle.

Have your partner toss a ball to you.

Catch the ball. Notice where your hand is. It probably is in front of you.

Do this a few times to lock in your muscle memory.

Problem: I hit the ball late.

Mistake: If you've played tennis, chances are you are taking a long backswing—that's okay in tennis, but that long stroke is not needed in pickleball as it wastes time and slows you down. A bigger backswing also can lead to hitting the ball late, which is why your ball flies out of bounds.

Solution: "You don't need a big backswing," said Coach M.J. "Stand sideways to a wall. Take your normal swing. Now move closer to the wall so your arm can't go that far back. Your muscle memory will realize where your swing should be."

Problem: The ball jams me.

Mistake: You run through the ball and hit the ball poorly.

Solution: "You need to be patient. Let the ball come to you. Don't rush into the ball. You have more time than you think to make the shot," said Coach Tim. "One of the best things you need to realize is to be patient and keep this whole game in front of you. Most of the time, we miss the ball when we've taken our eyes off the ball."

Problem: I'm out of position. The balls go by me.

Mistake: You might not be watching your opponent hitting the ball.

Solution: Read your opponent. Look at her paddle. Is she spinning the ball, trying for a lob, or slamming it back to you? Those hints show you where the ball will go and what it will do.

Problem: I get beaten by players much, much older than I am.

Mistake: Misjudging your opponent.

Solution: Don't overestimate or underestimate an opponent. Pickleball is a game of smarter, not harder.

Problem: My opponents hit shots I think are unreturnable.

Mistake: Easing up and not staying in ready position.

Solution: Always assume your opponent will return an unhittable shot. Some people have long legs or strong desires and will reach the ball. Stay prepared. Don't relax until your rally truly ends.

Watch This!

www.PickleballPublishingCompany.com/Top10BeginnerMistakes

Chapter 34
Pay It Forward

My first job was as a reporter for a newspaper in Florida. I saw the same story over and over.

A mid-level manager from Ohio enjoys being a big fish in a small pond. He has responsibilities. People report to him. He flirts with the waitress at the coffee shop. He feels important.

Then he retires to Florida. Everyone else who retired there was once a mid-level manager who had responsibilities and now has none. People didn't defer to him any longer. Waitresses didn't flirt with him.

He plays golf for a few weeks and gets bored. So, he drinks.

And drinks.

And drinks.

He is dead within five years because he has no social skills or friends.

If he's a scientist, he's dead within two years because scientists have even worse social skills than managers.

Women live much longer thanks to their bridge clubs, mahjong, and grandchildren. Women know how to make friends!

Let's be frank. There is a loneliness epidemic in America, especially among men. Men don't make friends outside of work. Men don't know how to make friends. Men die early because they have no social skills, no networks, and no friends.

Men make friends at work. But when the job ends, so do the friendships.

Men make friends with the parents of their kids' friends. But they wouldn't be friends if not for their kids. When the kids graduate, the friendships end because they really couldn't stand those people!

Is pickleball the answer?

Can pickleball bring people together?

I don't know. But it is a good start.

Pay It Forward

I'll never forget how out of place I felt when I went to my first pickleball open play session.

I had taken only two group lessons.

My instructor told me to go to "open play" to play against other people. He said it would be simple. You just go, pay your $6 fee, look for a group of people at your level, and "challenge" them by placing your paddle next to their net. After the match ended, the losers would leave, and you would play the winner with another challenger.

Sounded simple.

Until I got there.

Everyone was better than I was! After all, I had taken only two lessons! They had been playing for months or years!

I saw four women playing on one court. I figured they were besties and wouldn't want to play with a guy who wasn't part of their foursome.

I saw some young guys hitting the ball fast and hard. I could hardly see the ball! I couldn't play with them.

I was so new to pickleball that I didn't even know who was good and who was not!

So, I sat on a picnic table in the shade and watched people play for 30 minutes.

I was too afraid to put in my paddle and play against anyone!

After about half an hour, a woman came by and started chit-chatting. She noticed my San Francisco Giants cap and asked me if I was from there. She had relatives in San Francisco. We made light conversation. Then, she asked me if I wanted to play with her and her friends.

Finally! A breakthrough.

I told her I was new.

"We were all new players at one time," she said.

We played and had a good time. They didn't mind that I was a new player.

Since that day, I've heard that line many times from very nice people who play pickleball.

For the most part, my fears were unfounded. I learned not to jump to conclusions.

Myths came tumbling down!

I made incorrect assumptions on so many levels.

The four women who were playing together had never played together before! They welcomed the idea of a new player coming in so one of them could take a break. They were tired!

One of the four guys who hit lightning-fast balls had to leave early. They *needed* me so they could have enough people for a game!

Then I met Sandy. She wore a floppy gray hat, long sleeves, long pants, and gloves to protect her from the sun. She invited me to play with her and her friends. She told me a few tips to improve my game. She gently corrected me when I announced the wrong score (a common mistake for beginners).

The next time I played, I looked for Sandy. Her floppy hat was easy to spot. I walked to her court, and she welcomed me into the next game. We played together every week.

If it hadn't been for Sandy inviting me to play with her group, I probably never would have had the nerve to come back to the courts and play again. I might have slowly found a few other people to play against and gradually improved. Because she was so inviting week after week, I felt more comfortable coming to the courts. I'd look for her floppy hat and walk to her court. She welcomed me with a big smile. Her friends became my friends too.

If I hadn't met Sandy, I probably would have never played so many games, acquired so much knowledge, and written this book. And you wouldn't have this newfound information to boost your skills and confidence.

I hope you find your "Sandy" who welcomes you to join a new game.

Then, when you become comfortable playing, pay it forward.

Be a "Sandy."

I found my home.

You will too.

Before long, you'll make new friends who will be glad to see you. They will be sorry when you can't make a game!

I think back to Sandy, who welcomed me to pickleball. She paid it forward.

So do I.

I hope you do too.

You are now ready to practice these tips, techniques, and skills. Don't forget where you started.

Good luck!

Enjoy your journey!

Pickleball Gift Store

Do you like the cartoons in this book?

If so, did you know that all the cartoons in this book are available as t-shirts, coffee mugs, and more inside our Pickleball Gift Store?!

These one-of-a-kind products make perfect gifts for your pickleball partners, friends, and relatives! Or the perfect gift for yourself!

To learn more about our fun and exclusive gifts, visit: www.PickleBallPublishingCompany.com/gifts

Or visit cartoonist Lisa Rothstein's Etsy Store: www.etsy.com/shop/Rothtoons?section_id=43340850

Pickleball Products

Are you searching for the best equipment?

Check out our recommendations for superb products to enhance your pickleball journey!

From paddles to nets to clothing to court shoes, you'll find what you need at:

www.PickleBallPublishingCompany.com/products

"Pickleball Saved My Life!"

How many times have you said that?

Or heard people say that?

Probably lots of times!

Wouldn't it be great if your story inspired other people to take action to change their lives?

Now you can share your story in a new book called *Pickleball Saved My Life!*

Has pickleball helped you:

- Overcome loneliness and make new friends after losing a loved one or moving to a new area?

- Deal with depression, anxiety, or other issues by meeting new people and having something to look forward to?

- Lose weight, get in shape, or feel better?

- Find meaning in life by helping others get into the game, make friends, or build a community?

If so, you have a story to tell that can help people improve their lives.

You can share your inspirational short story in a new book, *Pickleball Saved My Life*. The book will be similar to the *Chicken Soup for the Soul* books.

If your story is selected, you'll get the following:

- Recognition as being an author!
- Ten free copies to give to your family and friends!

Your inspiring story could help people deal with their issues and get through their crises.

You can share your story—for free—and get copies of the books—for free—to give to your friends.

To share your story, go to

www.pickleballpublishingcompany.com/pages/pickleball-saved-my-life-share-your-story/

Share "Pickleball: The Ultimate Beginner's Guide to Fun, Friends, and Strategies" with Your Members!

Everyone wants to play pickleball!

Let's make it easy for you to help your clients, customers, and patrons get into the game—now!

You can build your brand—and your goodwill—when you order copies of this book to give away or sell to your members.

If you manage a country club, pickleball facility, bookstore, or sell pickleball merchandise, you can make money selling this book.

You can offer this book as a:

- Renewal premium

- New member drive

- Thank-you gift for long-standing members

- Recognition gift

- Profit center for your pro shop

The retail price of the book is $24.95. However, you can save money by ordering the book in bulk and either selling the book at a profit or giving the book away to build member loyalty.

Brand Your Business with a Book!

You can create a private-label version of *Pickleball: The Ultimate Beginner's Guide to Fun, Friends, and Strategies.* We can customize the cover to include the picture of your club. You can also include a one-page letter to your members. You can thank them for their patronage and highlight the benefits of membership, so they continue to renew.

If you manage a country club, pickleball facility, bookstore, or sell pickleball merchandise, you can make money selling *Pickleball: The Ultimate Beginner's Guide to Fun, Friends, and Strategies.*

For information, please set up an appointment with our sales team.

www.pickleballpublishingcompany.com/calendar

Or call Dan Janal at 651-605-5962 or email: publisher@PickleballPublishingCompany.com

There are several reasons why a private club might want to sell a book. Some potential benefits of selling books include:

Customer loyalty: books can foster a sense of community and connection among customers, which can lead to increased loyalty and repeat business.

Increased sales: books can be a profitable product for a retail store, especially if they are well-curated and selected to appeal to your target audience.

Brand image: selling books—or giving them away—can help to establish a club's image as a destination.

Overall, having your own customized version of *Pickleball: The Ultimate Beginner's Guide to Fun, Friends, and Strategies* can be a good

A way for a club to differentiate itself from competitors, attract members, and increase sales.

For information, call Dan Janal at 651-605-5962 or email: publisher@PickleballPublishingCompany.com

Acknowledgements

A big thank you to Tim Laurent, who knows everyone who is anyone in the pickleball world. Thank you for your introductions. This book wouldn't have been the same without you. I'm looking forward to future collaborations!

A terrific thank you to Lisa Rothstein, whose cartoons made you laugh and smile. There are many wonderful pickleball books out there, and standing out is hard. Lisa's cartoons are a brand differentiator. Did you know you can get t-shirts and mugs with those cartoons?

Go to www.pickleballpublishingcompany.com/store

Thanks to the people who offered editorial suggestions: Cathy Paper, Norm Brekke, Susan Tracy, Roberta Matuson, Marilyn Suey, Penny Hopkinson, Pat Iyer, Jeff Pike, Amy Suzanne Maeder, and Adam Hommey.

Thanks to the coaches who offered invaluable advice. They are all listed on the coaches' box at the beginning of the book. Check out their videos and their services.

About the Author
Dan Janal

Dan Janal is an avid pickleball player and the president of the Pickleball Publishing Company. Dan is also an inspirational, motivational speaker who delivers keynotes at conferences and on podcasts.

He is an award-winning journalist and author of more than a dozen books on a variety of business topics. He lives in Minneapolis and San Diego with his wife and two cats. He earned bachelor's and master's degrees in journalism from Northwestern University.

He also helps business people write their books as a ghostwriter, book coach, and developmental editor. For information go to http://www.WriteYourBookInAFlash.com.

He is a frequent guest on podcasts. Podcasters can invite him to appear on their shows by going to
www.pickleballpublishingcompany.com

Founded in 2022, Pickleball Publishing Company publishes books for the pickleball community. Current titles include

Pickleball: The Ultimate Beginner's Guide to Fun, Friends, and Strategies and *Pickleball Saved My Life* (summer 2023). PPC also produces the *Pickleball Saved My Life Podcast with Dan Janal*.

About the Cartoonist
Lisa Rothstein

Lisa Rothstein is a cartoonist whose work has appeared in *The New Yorker Magazine*, *Cybercrime Magazine*, and books including, *How To Survive Your Freshman Year (6th Edition)* and *One Coin, Two Coin, What Coin? Bitcoin!*

As a visual strategist and graphic facilitator, Lisa has worked with the Ladies Pro Golf Association (LPGA), LinkedIn, Chick-fil-A, the RSA Cybersecurity Conference, and many more. Lisa also teaches a popular workshop, *Drawing Out Your Genius™: Visual Thinking for Communication, Collaboration, Creative Thinking and Culture* that unlocks the hand-drawn communication skills of business leaders, innovators, and consultants. She's delivered this workshop to the Adobe 99U Conference, the BackEnd of Innovation, Innolead's Impact Conference, ATD conferences, Forbes Business Council, and to innovation teams at Bayer, Merck, and Rheem.

Previously, Lisa had a two-decades-long career as an associate creative director for ad agencies in New York and Europe on brands like IBM and Hanes. She divides her time between San Diego and her hometown of New York City.

For information, go to Drawingoutyourgenius.com

Made in the USA
Monee, IL
16 April 2024